Advanced
Lapidary Techniques

Advanced Lapidary Techniques

Herbert Scarfe

B.T. Batsford Limited   London

© Herbert Scarfe 1979
First published 1979
ISBN 0 7134 0398 5

Filmset in 'Monophoto' Imprint by
Servis Filmsetting Limited, Manchester

Printed and bound in Great Britain by
The Anchor Press Ltd, Tiptree, Essex
for the Publishers
B.T. Batsford Limited
4 Fitzhardinge St
London W1H 0AH

Contents

Acknowledgment

I am indebted to my wife, Doreen, for her assistance in the preparation of this book, also to Eric Johnson of Hull for taking photographs of the working sequences.

Special thanks are due to manufacturers and suppliers of lapidary equipment for their courtesy and help, particularly to the following for photographs of machines: Highland Park Manufacturing, Hawthorne, California, USA, figure 1. Lynhill Lapidary Ltd, Galashiels, Scotland, figure 2. Griffin & George Ltd, Wythenshawe, Manchester, England, figures 3, 5 and 6. Gemstones Ltd, Hull, England, figures 64 and 76. H.C. Evans & Son, London, England, figures 4 and 63. Diamond Pacific Tool Corporation, Barstow, California, USA, figure 7. D. Sustrik Enterprises Ltd, Edmonton, Alberta, Canada, figures 8, 9 and 10. Hirsh Jacobson Merchandising Co. Ltd, London, England, figure 77. Glenjoy Lapidary Supplies, Wakefield, England, figure 78. Kernowcraft Rock & Gems Ltd, Truro, Cornwall, England, figure 15. Ultra-Tec; Stanley Lapidary Products, Santa Ana, California, USA, figure 75.

Part One

Materials and Techniques

Fig 1 Highland Park 15 cm (6 in) Combination Unit. Saw, double grinder with overhead water coolant, drum sander on right.
Highland Park Manufacturing, Hawthorne, California, USA.

Fig 2 P.M.R.3 Combination Unit. Slab/trim saw, double grinder, sander, polisher. Overhead coolant tank.
Lynhill Lapidary Ltd, Galashiels, Scotland.

I   Machines and Materials

Most readers of a book on advanced lapidary techniques will already be familiar with methods of sawing, dopping and cutting standard cabochons but it is recognized that beginners to the craft and those with only slight experience will also be searching for advancement in their hobby. As a brief refresher on basic methods of preparation and cutting, together with a mention of different types of equipment and its uses, this chapter will set the scene for later advanced projects and be of value to lapidaries at all standards of attainment.

Lapidary machines perform the functions of sawing, grinding, sanding and polishing, and can be designed either to combine all of these in one unit or to fulfil various single requirements. While it may be preferable to have a number of single-purpose machines the choice may depend largely on the amount of workshop space available, also the cost, and for those who require a compact multi-purpose machine a combination unit will provide the answer (figures 1–10).

Differences in machine construction, for example either vertical or horizontal mounting for wheels and discs, have a direct influence on cutting techniques. Manipulative skills are acquired through practice and contact with materials and other physical factors will determine a personal approach. What does remain constant, irrespective of the machine used, is the sequence of cutting; a stone has to be sawn in the preparatory stages, ground into shape through a series of abrasive processes using grinding wheels, and followed by other forms of surface abrasion, usually referred to as sanding, to prepare the stone for polishing.

ABRASIVES

Silicon carbide is recognized as being a most suitable abrasive for general lapidary work and is made up in various forms which are associated with cabochon cutting machines. Lapidary grinding wheels are vitreous-

Fig 3 Gemtek 'Universal', 15 cm (6 in) saw, grinder, sanding and polishing unit. Water coolant supplied from trough under wheel.
Gemstones Ltd, Hull, England.

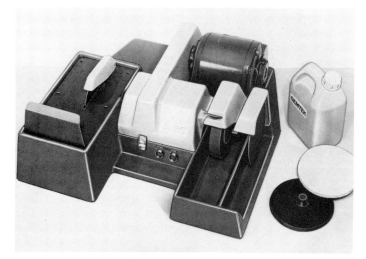

Fig 4 Evans SS12, 30 cm (12 in) slab saw with automatic three speed feed.
H.C. Evans & Son, Sidcup, England.

Fig 5 Gemtek 25 cm (10 in) slab saw with gravity feed.
Gemstones Ltd, Hull, England.

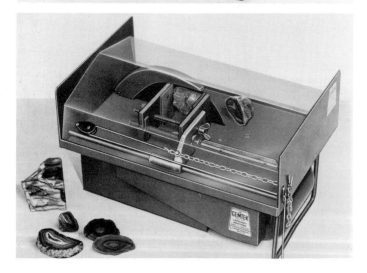

Fig 6 Gemtek 'Duo'. Double-ended grinding, sanding and polishing unit.
Gemstones Ltd, Hull, England.

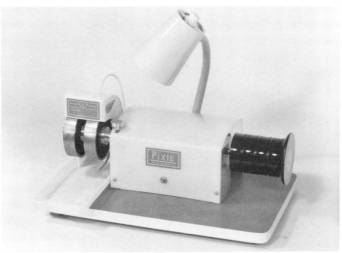

Fig 7 'Pixie' all diamond cabochon unit. Galaxy metal-bonded diamond wheels.
Diamond Pacific Tool Corp., Barstow, California, USA.

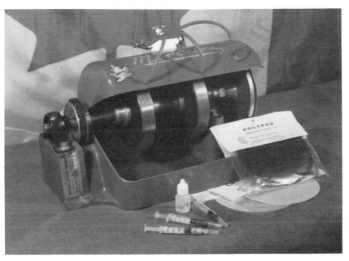

Fig 8 Mercury cabochon cutting unit. Diamond syringe applicators in foreground.
D. Sustrik Enterprises Ltd, Edmonton, Alberta, Canada.

Fig 9 Mercury lapidary unit with belt sander.
D. Sustrik Enterprises Ltd, Edmonton, Alberta, Canada.

Fig 10 Mercury belt sander as separate unit.
D. Sustrik Enterprises Ltd, Edmonton, Alberta, Canada.

bonded compositions of graded silicon carbide grits and ceramic materials. For sanding purposes there is a variety of coated abrasive surfaces such as flat discs of paper or cloth, as well as continuous belts or sleeves for drum sanders. Loose powdered grits are used on horizontal lapping plates for sanding flat sections and the grit sizes generally used are: 80 or 100 (very coarse), 220 and 320 (medium), 400 (fine) and 500 and 600 (very fine).

Diamond abrasives are increasing in popularity for cabochon cutting processes and are available as metal-bonded diamond wheels and channelled or ripple-surface discs. Pastes containing diamond particles are applied to supports of grooved hardwood and phenolic fibre laps and rolls. These abrasives are fast-cutting, clean in use, and will eliminate many of the problems of undercutting on stones with hard and soft areas that are sometimes experienced with silicon carbide.

Grinding wheels with the peripheral surface composed of sintered metal and diamond grits are used in much the same way as other types of wheels for pre-forming cabochon shapes, with water applied as a coolant. Differences arise at the sanding and polishing stages where, for example, the appropriate laps have to be charged with graded diamond pastes as needed. Some machines have a series of rolls with concave surfaces especially formed for sanding cabochons and other rounded stones. A separate roll is used for each progressively finer grade of diamond used (*see* table of grit sizes and micron mesh comparisons on page 74). Grooved hardwood laps are also used in conjunction with diamond for sanding rounded cabochon domes. The wood is made impervious to water by applications of light oil and wax which is worked well into the grooves. The waxed surface also helps to retain the diamond grit. Hardwood laps are manufactured which have been impregnated with special resin preparations capable of holding fine diamond particles when charged.

Other aids to sanding with diamond pastes include an assortment of small tubes that can be screwed to the central spindle of horizontal lapidary units. Copper cups are secured in the tubes and these are then charged with diamond. The dopstick is held in a vertical position during sanding, working the stone against the cup as the tube rotates. Dish-shaped or channelled discs of metal with diamond embedded in the surface are featured on some machines and these have a drip feed tube supplying water coolant to the work. Resin-bonded diamond laps, discs and peripheral wheel surfaces add to the extensive range of products available for processing cabochons and flat sections, enabling the cutter to employ diamond techniques throughout all stages of cutting and polishing.

CHARGING ROLLS AND LAPS WITH DIAMOND

Diamond pastes are supplied in syringe applicators each with the manufacturer's colour coding to denote the micron size of the diamond particles. A very small quantity of paste goes a long way and a single charging will remain effective for sanding many cabochons before replenishment is needed. As a guide, the larger micron sizes 45, 30, 15 are used for sanding stones to a pre-polish state and the smaller sizes, 3 and 1, for polishing. Extender fluids are available for thinning diamond compounds when used on rigid surfaces and these help to spread the particles over the lap. But as the compound itself acts as a lubricant it is necessary to add only a little extender when excessive dragging is felt.

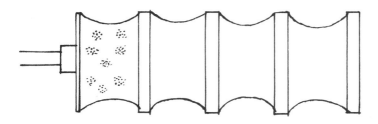

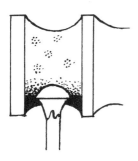

Fig 11 Diamond compound applied to rolls and spread with dopped stone.

To charge concave rollers with diamond, small dots of compound are applied at evenly spaced intervals around the rolls which can be made of wood or toughened masonite. Use a smooth dopped stone to spread the diamond particles, gradually turning the rolls by hand until all the compound is distributed over the surface (figure 11).

Machine units for sanding, similar to those shown in figure 12, have a series of interchangeable phenolite discs which can be charged with diamond by pressure from a hard composition roller. Padded discs are used for polishing and these are glued into position with a peel-off type of adhesive for easy renewal when necessary. Fine micron compound is smeared on the polishing discs and spread with the fingertips.

Fig 12 Sanding and polishing unit with diamond. The 'Diamond Miser'.
Ran-co Products, Granada Hills, California, USA.

To charge grooved hardwood laps apply six to eight spots of the required micron size compound around the grooves. Spread evenly with the fingers and embed the particles into the wood with a dopped cabochon, turning the lap by hand.

It is not necessary to run diamond laps at fast speeds and it is advisable to follow the manufacturer's recommendations for the product. As a rough guide it is suggested that for cutting cabochons with diamond a speed between 1000 and 2000 rpm is sufficient for most stones but for harder gem materials the polishing stage can be performed at about 750 rpm.

POLISHES

A variety of polishing agents is available such as cerium oxide, tin oxide, chrome oxide and aluminium oxide preparations such as Linde A. Separate laps must be kept for each type of oxide used and these can be of felt, leather or waxed muslin. The padded muslin lap must be coated with beeswax worked well in to give a smooth surface.

Very fine diamond compound is also used in producing highly polished surfaces on cabochons and the laps used can be grooved hardwood, resin-bonded pads or leather, with a rubber or other resilient backing to cushion the curvature of the stone.

DOPPING

The process of dopping a stone to facilitate handling is one of the skills acquired at an early stage of cabochon cutting. There are several methods of dopping but the selected technique of mounting a stone on a stick should ensure a firm and tidy support that will remain in position for as long as required.

Warm dopping is a widely used process, incorporating heating appliances for melting wax and heating stones. Dopping wax is a mixture of sealing wax, powdered shellac and a little beeswax but can be obtained ready-made from lapidary dealers.

Cold dopping is used primarily for heat-sensitive stones and a cement is easily made from cornflour and clear acetone adhesive. Only small quantities need be mixed together in a firm dough that is moulded on the end of a dopstick. A smear of acetone glue at the base of the stone will provide a good bond with the supporting dough. Allow it to set hard before shaping the stone. Acetone or an acetone-based solvent will remove the stone from the dop by a short period of immersion.

For those who prefer to dispense with heating appliances and use a cold dopping method for all types of stones there are branded makes of cold dop adhesive, consisting of two coloured strips of epoxy in putty form that are kneaded together then used to dop stones in the usual way. It is then necessary to wait about 20 minutes before starting to cut the stone.

Another method of cold dopping uses heavy-duty double-sided adhesive tape on a shaped metal or plastic dop with a smooth surface. The advantages of this dopping method are minimal waiting time before starting cutting and ease of removal when completed.

DRILLING HOLES IN STONES

The most effective drill tips are of diamond, either sintered to a metal shank or electroplated in a single layer. Sintered drills have a greater depth of diamond and with careful use have a more prolonged cutting life. With either type of drill excessive pressures exerted on the tips will impair efficiency through wear and loss of particles on the point. For this reason correct techniques and continuous contact with coolant fluid are essential to prevent damage and over-heating since the drills operate at high speeds.

Drill bits of different diameters are made to fit interchangeable chucks of either battery- or mains-operated small hand drills which can also be fixed in a drill stand. For drilling soft stones fine metal twist drills can be employed.

To secure a stone for drilling, press it firmly into a bed of plasticine in the bottom of a shallow dish. Add sufficient water to cover the stone as a coolant and also to provide a flushing action at the drill tip to clear the hole of obscuring particles (figure 13). During drilling apply only enough pressure to feel the bite of the drill penetrating the stone and raise the drill every few seconds to clear the tip. Where the stone is of a brittle nature a piece of masking tape stuck on the underside will help to prevent the edges of the hole crumbling as the drill breaks through. Alternatively, drill half way then reverse the stone to drill from the other side until the holes meet.

The initial stages of drilling down onto a curved surface, as in the case of pendants and heart shapes, may present difficulties with the drill tip slipping down the curve and scratching the stone. This is a greater hazard if the stone has a highly glazed surface and where possible the final polishing stage should be postponed

until the hole has been drilled. To overcome the problem of slipping, raise the end of the stone by pushing it into the plasticine at an angle, making sure it is supported all round to prevent movement. This will allow the drill to pierce the stone at the required point and give a foothold for continued drilling. As the direction of the hole at this angle may be too steep, once the indentation has been made the stone can be laid flat to complete the drilling.

Fig 13 Drilling a stone with small battery-powered drill.

2 Cabochon Stones

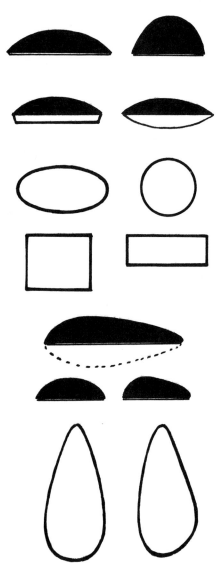

Fig 14 Some cabochon styles. Perimeter and profile shapes.

The term *cabochon* is now loosely used for any non-faceted stone and is characterized by rounded polished surfaces cut by hand. A dome can be high or low, with either symmetrical or irregular profile, and changes in perimeter shape also add to the many variations (figure 14). Orthodox cabochons cut for standard jewellery settings are usually flat on one side with a gentle curve springing from a round or oval shape to form a shallow dome. For competition purposes the ideal standard cabochon should have a maximum height of dome not exceeding 50 percent of the shortest axis of the outline shape and have a back bevel. The oval cabochon is perhaps the most popular cut of all; favoured by the beginner as an introduction to each lapidary process and by the more advanced cutter in pursuit of increasing skills in precision and excellence of finish.

The cabochon style of cutting is generally more suited to opaque and translucent gem minerals which possess the attractions of colour, pattern and lustre. Other unique properties in a stone's structure can show such qualities as iridescence, chatoyancy and asterism in correctly orientated cabochons. Hardness, or resistance to abrasion, is shown by numerical grading from one to ten based on Mohs' scale which indicates the ability of a mineral to scratch others of a softer composition. It should be noted that many stones in the same mineral grouping may vary in hardness to some extent and this is particularly evident in gems of the quartz family though all are shown as seven on Mohs' scale. Hardness should not be confused with degrees of toughness, where the cohesive structure of a stone determines its breaking point, for example brittle to extreme toughness. Comparative scales of hardness are given in the appendices.

The following list of stones will give some idea of the wide range of materials for cutting that are available through lapidary dealers or in some countries can be found in their natural environment.

Agate Varieties Cryptocrystalline quartz	Hardness 7 (Mohs' scale)
Banded, fortification, orbicular	White to pale blue chalcedony with red, brown, black, green or yellow banding or circular patterns.
Moss agate	Translucent chalcedony with green, red, or brown moss-like inclusions
Dendritic or tree agate	White to pale brown, opaque. Dendritic inclusions of green, brown or black resembling tree growth
Plume and flame agate	Translucent. Fused colouration suggesting feathers or smoke and flames
Scenic agate	Opaque – translucent. Inclusions suggest landscape features
Lace agate	Opaque – translucent. Finely banded in intricate lacy patterns
Amazonite Microcline feldspar	Hardness 6 Pale to medium turquoise green. Schiller effect when correctly orientated
Amber Organic – fossilized resin	Hardness $2\frac{1}{2}$ Lemon yellow to orange-brown, red. Translucent – opaque
Aventurine Crystalline quartz	Hardness 7 Light to deep green, blue, orange. Translucent. Contains silvery flecks of mica or haematite
Chalcedony Varieties Cryptocrystalline quartz	Hardness $6\frac{1}{2}$–7
Bloodstone	Opaque. Dark green spotted with red. Brittle
Carnelian	Translucent. Orange to red
Chalcedony	Milky white to pale blue
Chrysoprase	Translucent. Bright green
Jasper	Opaque. Chalcedony fused with coloured oxides. Red, green, yellow to brown
Onyx	Opaque. Layered white, black and grey
Plasma	Opaque. Dark green
Sard	Opaque. Red-brown
Sardonyx	Opaque. Layered red-brown and white

Fluorite (Fluorspar)
variety: Blue John

Hardness 4
Translucent. Light to dark purple with white or yellow banding

Haematite
Iron Oxide

Hardness $5\frac{1}{2}$–6
Black with metallic lustre

Howlite
Calcium boro-silicate

Hardness 3
Opaque. White, white with black veins

Jade
Nephrite

Hardness 6–$6\frac{1}{2}$
Opaque. White, light to dark green.

Jadeite

Hardness $6\frac{1}{2}$–7
Opaque. Green to blue-green, mauve, brown, red.

Jet
Organic – fossil wood

Hardness $2\frac{1}{2}$–3
Opaque. Intense black. Compact

Labradorite
Plagioclase feldspar

Hardness 6
Opaque. Dark blue-grey. Displays spectrum colours when viewed in different positions due to lamellar twinning

Lapis Lazuli
Lazurite

Hardness 5–$5\frac{1}{2}$
Opaque. Ultramarine blue flecked with pyrite

Malachite
Copper carbonate

Hardness 3–4
Opaque. Deep to pale green with ribbon and orbicular banding

Moonstone
Orthoclase feldspar

Hardness 6–$6\frac{1}{2}$
Translucent. Colourless, whitish to blue. Displays moving band of light on surface

Obsidian
Volcanic glass

Hardness 5
Opaque, translucent. Intense black to mahogany brown. Colour can be evenly distributed or striped; smoky brown and rainbow sheen. With inclusions of white or grey known as snowflake obsidian. Brittle

Opal
Hydrated silica

Hardness $5\frac{1}{2}$–$6\frac{1}{2}$
Amorphous. Precious opal shows play of spectrum colours varying in intensity. Heat sensitive

Petrified Wood
many varieties

Opaque. Mineral replacement of wood by agate, jasper opal. Hardness according to composition

Quartz Crystalline varieties	Hardness 7
Rock crystal	Transparent. Colourless, water-clear
Rose quartz	Translucent. Pale pink
Amethyst	Transparent to translucent. Purple, sometimes with colour zoning or white banding
Citrine	Transparent. Pale to deep yellow
Smoky quartz	Transparent. Light to dark brown
Rhodochrosite Manganese carbonate	Hardness 4 Opaque – translucent. Pale pink to red with white. Satin sheen
Rhodonite Manganese silicate	Hardness 5–6 Opaque. Pale pink to deep red veined with black
Rutilated Quartz Crystalline quartz	Hardness 7 Transparent with inclusions of golden rutile needles. Colourless or smoky brown
Sodalite Sodium aluminium silicate	Hardness $5\frac{1}{2}$–6 Opaque. Light to deep blue streaked with white or grey
Tiger's Eye (Crocidolite) Silicified asbestos	Hardness 7 Opaque. Golden yellow to brown, blue to green. If heat treated – red. Chatoyant
Thulite Zoisite	Hardness 6–7 Opaque. Deep pink
Tourmaline in Quartz Crystalline quartz	Hardness 7 Transparent. Colourless with needle-like inclusions of black tourmaline
Variscite Aluminium phosphate	Hardness $4\frac{1}{2}$–5 Light green to blue green. Vitreous lustre

Different kinds of material become available as lapidary dealers are continually importing stones from many parts of the world and this is by no means an exhaustive list of material for cutting.

STAGES IN CUTTING CABOCHONS

Preparation : Slabbing. Saw blades 20 cm (8 in) diameter upwards. Rock clamp should be used.

(a) Section slabbed from rock.

(b) Uneven rock set in plaster of Paris to assist clamping.

Trimming. Saw blades up to 20 cm (8 in) diameter.

(c) Slab divided for most economical use, to plan cabochon blanks.

(d) Allowance to be made for wastage and thickness of saw blade.

Marking out. Pierced templates or adhesive shapes.

(e) Aluminium marker with sharp point. Hold at an angle to draw into edge of template shape.

(f) Adhesive 'peel-off' template shape placed on stone.

Pre-forming oval blank.

(g), (h) Trim saw used as aid to remove material and save grinding.

(h) Parallel cuts can be levered away.

(i) Oval base ground to shape on wheel. Aluminium mark should still be visible.

Bevel on base rim.

(j) A fine bevel cut on rim of pre-form base. Base and side section views.

(k) Stone dopped bevel side down.

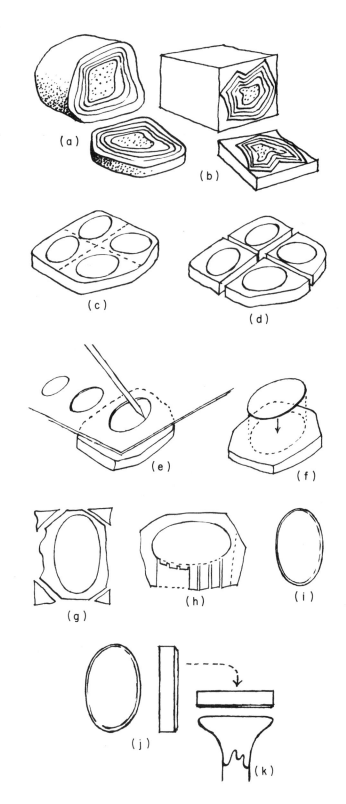

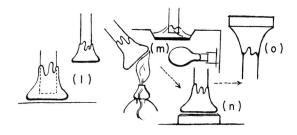

Dopping
(l) Prepare dop sticks with cone of wax.
(m) Heating wax in flame; alternatively dowel dipped in tray of electrically heated wax.
(n) Wax pressed down onto heated stone.
(o) Wax moulded firmly to support stone.

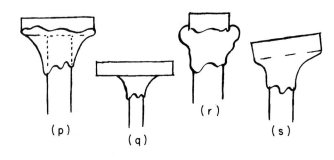

Dopping faults.
(p) End of dopstick should not be in contact with stone. Surplus wax must be removed from stone to prevent wavy edge on stone when cut.
(q) Dopstick too narrow for width of stone.
(r) Dopstick too large; stone embedded in surplus wax.
(s) Stone dopped off-centre. This will result in irregular shaped cabochon.

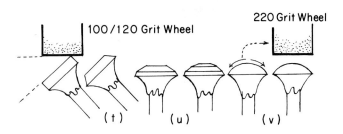

Shaping the dome : Use of grinding wheels. Water coolant.
(t) First bevel cut at approximately 45 degrees to wheel front.
(u) Changing angles to give a series of step cut bevels.
(v) Refinement of shape on finer grinding wheels.

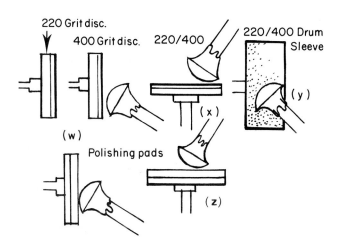

Sanding and polishing. Sanding discs or sleeves for drum sander of wet/dry paper or cloth.
Polishing pads of leather or felt.
(w) Sanding and polishing on end mounted vertical discs.
(x) Sanding and polishing on horizontal discs.
(y) Drum sander.
(z) Vertical and horizontal polishing.

Fig 15 Horizontal saw and rock clamp.

Fig 16 Use of vertical trim saw.

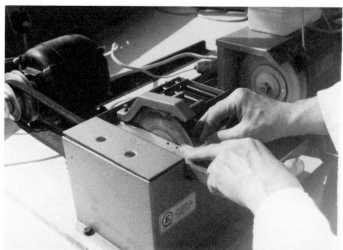

Fig 17 Dopping appliances, *left* – electrically heated hot plate, *right* – spirit lamp and inverted can. *Front* – prepared dopsticks.

Fig 18 Shaping a cabochon dome.

Fig 19 Sanding on wet/dry disc with water coolant applied as necessary.

3   Special Treatments

Many of the stones that require special care and treatment to obtain a good finish occur in the lower hardness range, particularly where their composition includes hard and soft minerals. Failure to attain a high polish may often be the result of inadequate sanding in the earlier stages or the wrong choice of lap and polishing medium. In some cases sanding and polishing techniques will need adjustment to suit a particular stone. It must be emphasized that the quality of polish expected from the range of gem minerals cut as cabochons or flat lapped sections will vary considerably between a highly reflective finish and a rather dull lustre.

Careful choice of rough can eliminate many problems from the outset; for best results reject any materials showing fractures and fine cracks, also check for any obvious signs of weakness in stones with known pronounced cleavage. Badly pitted surfaces often give rise to doubts about the depth of the imperfections; this is also true of surface areas with unwanted inclusions or veins of impure material. Tests can be made by grinding carefully to determine whether the imperfections are only shallow and easily removed or penetrate the stone to greater depth.

It is important to know the degree of porosity in the selected rough as this can affect the choice of coolant liquids for slabbing and trimming. Very porous material should not be cut with oil or oil-based preparations as rapid saturation will alter the original colouration and lessen the chances of a good finish. Where oil is used in any cutting process it is recommended that the stone is placed in a bowl of warm water and detergent immediately after sawing. Alternatively, stones can be put in a container of fine sawdust or absorbent granules to soak out the oil.

Identification of gem rough is an important factor and knowledge of qualities such as hardness, cleavage and composition will indicate the stone's reaction to stresses of heat and prolonged abrasion. From this understanding a more confident selection of appropriate cutting and finishing processes can be made.

Owing to structural characteristics, many stones possess special optical qualities requiring careful orientation during cutting. The descriptive terms to associate some of these unique values include *asterism* in stones displaying rayed star formations; *adularescence* referring to silvery and soft bluish bands of light as, for example, in moonstones; *chatoyancy*, silky bands of moving light reflected from a fine fibrous structure in the material; *iridescence*, displays of colour or sheen reflected from translucent layered films as seen in iris agate and rainbow obsidian; *opalescence*, a milky effect due to scattering of light from small particles in the stone, seen in common opal; *schiller*, planes of reflected light from cleavage layers, displayed by many of the feldspars, for example amazonite and sunstone, while labradorite shows an iridescent sheen.

Cutting characteristics and suggested treatments for the following materials will offer a solution to some of the problems likely to be encountered when using standard cabochon cutting equipment and silicon carbide abrasives. With diamond abrasives and finishes many of these difficulties will not occur and techniques are simplified.

INORGANIC MATERIALS
Quartz H.7

Stones within this mineral group usually respond well to orthodox treatment and with only one or two exceptions, present few problems. Insufficient water coolant during grinding and sanding produces overheating and is the principal danger to quartz gems, causing surface flaking and internal fractures. The crystalline varieties have a greater tendency to chip during grinding than the more compact chalcedony material.

Troublesome stones include moss agate, where occasionally the dendritic inclusions break through the surface, showing a network of minute cavities. These become more pronounced when filled with dried polishing oxides. Slight imperfections can often be removed by meticulous sanding during the various grit stages using copious water coolant and the cutter must be prepared to repeat the process until an improved surface is formed. The same treatment should be applied to Tiger's eye where ends of the fibrous structure tend to break through the surface of domed cabochons. Very coarse and twisted fibres defy a smooth finish and careful slabbing and orientation of the stone may avoid some of these difficulties, but selecting good quality material with finely packed silky fibres is an important consideration.

Jaspers, with coloured clays and often metallic minerals infused into the silica groundmass, are susceptible to undercutting. This frequently occurs at the polishing stage when using felt discs and where the softer minerals are dragged from the material through frictional heat. A leather lap with cerium oxide is less severe and will give improved results.

Chalcedony has a purer silica content, for example the translucent white to clear blue and red carnelian varieties, and is sensitive to heat and vibration from bumpy grinding wheels which are badly worn or running out of true. Extreme care and light pressures must be used with adequate water coolant to prevent fractures. Agate slabs and nodule sections, also with high chalcedony content, respond well to lapping with slurries of loose grits and will take a flawless polish providing each stage has been carried out thoroughly.

Jade (Nephrite H.6–$6\frac{1}{2}$, Jadeite H.$6\frac{1}{2}$–7)

During sanding and polishing both types of jade are subject to surface roughening or formation of orange-skin texture. To achieve success liberally apply water coolant during the preliminary sanding stages both to avoid over-heating and to counteract any drag on the surface of the silicon carbide discs. The vital stages take place on a well-worn 600 disc. Continue sanding wet using moderate pressure at the start, gradually allow the disc to dry out and increase pressure on the stone until smooth glazing occurs. Repeat this action if necessary, commencing wet. Final polishing is carried out on a soft leather lap with chrome oxide, or a mixture of chrome oxide and Linde A, using heavy pressure.

Feldspars (Amazonite, Labradorite, Moonstone, Sunstone)

Success here depends on good material and careful orientation to take advantage of the schiller effects. Orientation prior to cutting can be assisted by wetting the stone and holding under a concentrated light source. By moving the stone in different directions the characteristic displays of schiller and colour can be located.

Layered structure and easy cleavage require the stones to be worked with gentle pressures and a good supply of coolant, avoiding vibration and over-heating. Check the orientation repeatedly under a light and make allowances for adjustment during cutting. The play of light in moonstone can be positioned in the centre of a high-domed cabochon as a central spot or as an elongated band in a more shallow-cut stone. Sand very wet and proceed gradually to a pre-polish stage on a well-worn 600 sanding disc. Complete the polish with cerium oxide on a felt lap, taking care not to over-heat.

Lapis Lazuli H.5–5$\frac{1}{2}$

The quality of polish will form as a sheen rather than a high-gloss finish. The dull blue lustre contrasts with shiny golden flecks of pyrites which are present in good-quality material. Undercutting is likely to occur in any white or grey areas found in inferior grades. This is a relatively soft stone requiring careful shaping and wet sanding using moderate to gentle pressures. Avoid excessive frictional heat at any stage and polish on leather with a paste of tin oxide or chrome oxide.

Opal H.5$\frac{1}{2}$–6$\frac{1}{2}$

Owing to its porosity opal should be trimmed with a thin diamond saw blade using water coolant only. Moisture is an essential factor in retaining opal in good condition and dehydration through frictional heat places the material in a critical and brittle state. Ensure that the stone is cut and sanded wet at each stage and grind at slower speeds on a 220 wheel with delicacy and lightness of handling since the rate of abrasion is rapid. Orientation for colour should be made in easy stages before the final cabochon shape is established. Sand on worn 400 and 600 sanding discs and polish on leather with cerium oxide.

Obsidian H.5

This is a brittle material which tends to flake and chip during preparatory grinding stages if pressures are excessive or over-heating occurs. Protection for the eyes is suggested when using a trim saw on obsidian for it is among the worst offenders for throwing up minute particles of sharp fragments.

Once the basic shaping has been achieved little further trouble will be encountered and the stone will polish rapidly to a high-gloss finish using cerium oxide on a felt lap. Cabochons cut from rainbow obsidian displaying an iridescent sheen need to be orientated carefully. Examine wet in a good light to place the areas of colour or iridescent banding most effectively in the cabochon dome.

Grossular Garnet H.7$\frac{1}{4}$

Often termed grossularite or 'Transvaal jade' from South Africa, this massive green variety of garnet produces attractive cabochons and works well through the usual stages of sanding and polishing. Despite its apparent toughness it has a tendency to chip during sawing and grinding, particularly if over-heating occurs. As the material is very dense in composition and finely structured, sawing operations are prolonged owing to lack of 'bite' by the saw blade. This is where dangers of over-heating are likely to build up and it is essential when slabbing to ensure that the coolant level in the saw tank is adequate.

Rhodochrosite H.4

This is an absorbent stone so use water coolant in preference to oily substances for sawing. During grinding removal of material is rapid owing to softness and a wheel run at half normal grinding speed is preferable. Gentle pressure is needed as the stone is structurally weak along lines of banding and is susceptible to parting if subjected to harsh treatment. Sand wet on worn discs as new abrasive surfaces are too severe. Pre-polish on 600 grit or finer and polish on leather with tin oxide.

Malachite H.3–4

Malachite dust is toxic if inhaled over prolonged periods and the stone should never be cut dry. Dangers are minimized by using copious water coolant at each stage and washing both the stone and hands thoroughly at the end of each session. Rinse the green residue from grinding wheels before cutting stones of different materials.

Highly absorbent, malachite must be sawn with water and not oily coolants as these cause darkening of the colour and tend to reduce a potentially good polish to a dull lustre.

Cut on fine wheels and sand wet on 400 to 600 sanding discs. Polish on leather with a water-based slurry of chrome oxide or tin oxide, adding a few drops of vinegar to the solution. As a final process the stone can be rubbed by hand on a soft leather pad with a thin mixture of polish and detergent.

ORGANIC MATERIALS
Jet H.3$\frac{1}{2}$ and Amber H.2$\frac{1}{2}$

Materials of organic origin react quickly to abrasion and

require delicacy of handling when worked on powered equipment. Despite their softness jet and amber are tough, compact materials capable of high polish.

As shaping is rapid it should be done on either a 220 wheel or a new 220 sanding disc with plenty of water coolant. Jet is messy to work and the accumulation of brown slurry will need frequent rinsing from both the work and abrasive surfaces. Both jet and amber are heat-sensitive but adequate coolant will prevent burning and formation of crackled surfaces. Pre-polish on 400 to 600 worn sanding discs, starting wet and allowing to run dry. Further polishing can be done on a soft leather lap with cerium oxide, or rubbed by hand on a velvet pad or dry chamois leather.

With these materials the entire shaping and polishing can be done by hand, starting with wet/dry papers with moisture added and completing on a pad of soft leather with oxide slurries.

Kauri Gum H.2

This is a form of hardened copal resin from New Zealand which when cut and polished for jewellery is similar to amber in many ways. Techniques used for amber are applied to kauri gum but over-heating leads to problems of tackiness if coolant factors are neglected.

Abalone or Paua Shell H.3½–4

Although not difficult to work, special treatments are necessary during preparatory stages of work with this material. The rough outer shell layers can be removed either by filing or by coating with dilute solution of nitric acid and washing away the dissolved layers. To prevent further reaction on the shell the acid is neutral-ized with ammonia followed by thorough rinsing. Acid treatment should be done in the open air or a well-ventilated room to counteract unpleasant fumes and hands must be protected from acid solutions with rubber gloves.

Pre-forming can be done with hand tools such as hacksaws and files then sanding with wet/dry papers, but during these processes a face-mask or filter pad must be worn to prevent inhalation of noxious dust particles. The material polishes easily by rubbing vigorously on a soft pad with cerium oxide. Where powered equipment is used liberal water coolant must be added during grind-ing and sanding. Similar techniques are employed with other shells having a pearly lustre.

Coral H.3$\frac{1}{2}$

Pink and red corals cut and polish into attractive gem cabochons but owing to the limited solid areas, they are of very small dimensions. The composition of coral is basically calcium carbonate and the branching structure is extremely brittle.

Once the compact portions have been isolated from the perforated central core of the stems, cabochons are formed in the usual way. The material is easy to work and can be ground and sanded quite rapidly both by hand methods and using powered machines. Polish with tin oxide on leather.

TREATMENT OF UNDERCUT AND FLAWED SURFACES

Materials showing signs of undercutting and other surface flaws at the polishing stage, particularly those not normally associated with such traits, may require an alternative treatment. As already mentioned, felt laps exert considerable surface drag and generate heat that is often detrimental to the mineral structure of many gems.

If such flaws are present it will be necessary to return to sanding stages, the grades being determined by the severity of the surface flaws, until the stone is once again smooth. Examination of the surface through a magnifying lens will help to decide on the treatment required. In some instances repeated sanding may solve the problem. If a felt-polishing lap has already been used then change to a moistened leather lap and repolish with a slurry of suitable oxide. Invariably a better result will follow but it may even be necessary to try a different polishing agent, for example tin oxide might provide a better finish than cerium oxide, always on a separate lap.

Where flaws, inclusions and minute pores still persist these are often intensified through discolouration by polishing oxides. Several methods are employed to lessen the effects of ingrained polish during the actual polishing process. For short periods hard soap can be forced into pores and cracks to prevent penetration of polish. This is renewed as required and finally washed away. Paraffin wax is more suited to extended polishing sessions but should be thinned by heating and diluting with liquid paraffin. The warmed stone is dipped into the solution to fill the cracks and any surplus wax should be cleaned from the stone before resuming polishing.

A waterglass solution (sodium or potassium silicate) is also used to fill any imperfections and particularly useful when polishing moss agate and similar stones where inclusions or fibres break the surface. Immerse the stone and allow time for the solution to penetrate the undercut portions. Remove and allow to harden before polishing. On completion wash the stone in warm water.

Colourless epoxy resin is sometimes used for sealing imperfections by forcing it into cracks and pores. This method can be employed at the sanding stages if it becomes necessary and the hardened epoxy usually withstands abrasion and will present a smooth surface ready for polishing.

STAR STONES
Sapphire, Ruby, Rose Quartz, Garnet, Diopside.
Qualities of asterism in stones is best seen when the crystalline material is cut in hemispherical form or high dome cabochons. Not all stones will display stars of equal value or clarity and good formation depends on the concentration of reflective fibres within the crystal in right-angled planes to the crystallographic 'C' axis. The symmetry of the stars usually conforms to the particular crystal system of the gem mineral, for example in four or six radial light bands, or considerably more where twinned structural growth occurs. Stars formed in synthetic gem material are often more sharply defined.

Minerals which reveal asterism are usually translucent with pale to deep colouration and in many cases the fibrous structure or inclusions will not be visible to the naked eye. Round, high-domed cabochons will reflect a well balanced star while oval shaped cabochons will elongate the rays in one direction. It is quite usual for the stars to fade off at the ends.

Orientation
Where the crystal faces are still evident it should not be difficult to determine the position of the cabochon base which must be at right angles to the crystallographic 'C' axis (figure 20). In the case of an irregular gem rough the problem is not quite so simple. A number of trial faces will have to be rounded by smoothing out all points and hollows to the finer sanding stage until a satin sheen is formed. Polishing will aid the search even further if the star is not immediately evident.

Wet the stone or smear with refined oil and hold directly under a pinpoint light source. Move the stone about slowly until a single spot of light can be positively established in one position denoting the centre of the

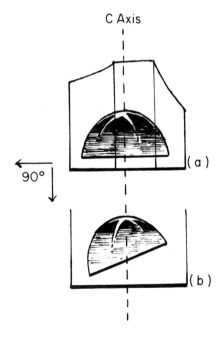

Fig 20 Orientation of star stones. (a) Cabochon base at right angles to 'c' axis of centred stone. (b) Star off-centre.

star. In some cases star rays may be visible around the curvature of the stone. Mark the position of the central spot of light or intersection of the light bands and this will be the top of the cabochon.

Cut the cabochon dome retaining as much height as possible and keeping the circle of light in a central position. Carry out repeated inspections under a light and be prepared to make minor adjustments during cutting. Level up the base and dop the stone if not done earlier and carry out sanding and polishing stages. Remove from the dop and polish the base. A reflective surface such as a mirror placed under the completed cabochon will sometimes intensify the star when light is reflected back through the stone.

CAT'S EYE STONE

Chrysoberyl, Quartz, Tourmaline, Tiger's eye (Croci-dolite).

Cat's eye stones are cut from minerals with fibrous or tubular inclusions (often invisible to the naked eye) which reflect a silky sheen known as chatoyancy when they are orientated in a particular way. This is seen as a moving band of light at right angles to the fibrous structure when the stone is cut as a cabochon.

When cutting, the base of the cabochon should lie parallel to the fibres and be so arranged that the chatoyant band runs in the direction of the longer dimension in an oval stone (figure 21). The cat's eye can be wide or narrowed to a thin line by adjusting the height and shape of the dome. In tiger's eye the fibrous inclusions should be fine and straight within the gem rough in order to centre a single cat's eye. Warping of the fibres leads to distortion and multiplication of the band of light. Single cat's eye gems can be cut from good quality tiger's eye and some of the best results are cut from the blue variety where the tonal contrasts are greater.

Orientation of cat's eye stones follows an almost identical procedure to that given for star stones but as the fibrous structure is often more evident the chatoyant bands are usually more well defined when moved under a light. By observing the structural pattern the cat's eye can be centred and the cabochon proportion worked out accordingly. Many of these stones are opaque or slightly translucent.

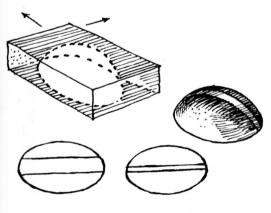

Fig 21 Orientation of cat's eye stone.

4 *Advanced Projects*

Cutting standard cabochons provides an excellent introduction to lapidary processes and the acquisition of skills. The beginner is also made aware of the characteristics of different gem minerals and the way they react under certain conditions of working. At some stage, however, progression beyond basic cabochon forms becomes necessary, not only for retention of interest but also to offer more challenging aspects of the craft. With this in view several advanced projects have been selected to incorporate the widest range of processes and utilize equipment in different ways. Most of the cutting sequences described refer to the use of machines designed for lapidary work with silicon carbide abrasives, since equipment of this kind is by far the most widespread and is sufficiently versatile to suit general requirements. For those who are using diamond cabochon cutting equipment a similar technique is employed.

DOUBLE CABOCHONS

Stones cut in this style can serve many purposes and often provide fresh incentives to those who design and make their own jewellery by combining particular shapes and qualities of stones with satisfactory solutions for mounting them. Perimeter shapes can be oval, round or square and in smaller sizes are suitable for setting in rings and bracelets. Pendants have similar geometric outlines but will include triangular to pear-shaped drops tapering towards the supporting end. Cutting these shapes as double cabochons, that is with a curve both above and below the girdle line, involves increased technical skill and demands good visual assessment of proportion and symmetry. Finished stones need not be of identical depths above and below the girdle and much will depend on the type of setting envisaged, although pendants with equal mass at front and rear will give a better balance when hanging from a chain.

Whatever stone is selected for a double cabochon the

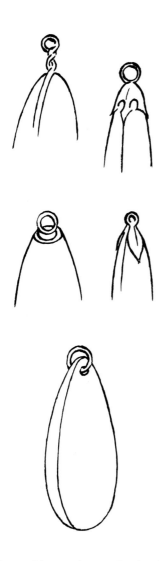

Fig 22 Alternative methods of hanging pendant shapes.

trimmed slab must be thicker than for its single counterpart, the depth being increased proportionately to the scale of the work. This will make full allowance for the double curvature and lessen the problem of flat areas occurring at the centre of the domes.

Cutting a Double Pendant

This has been selected as a good technical exercise in cutting and polishing identical halves. The completed stone also lends itself to different ways of hanging, one of which introduces a method of cutting a continuous groove around the girdle using a trim saw. The method described involves the use of silicon carbide on a standard lapidary machine but the techniques can be adapted for use with diamond equipment.

First decide on a pendant shape, for example wide at the lower end and tapering in a gentle curve towards the top. The method to be used for hanging the finished pendant, either by fixing a bell cap or drilling a hole for insertion of a jump ring, will determine the size of the taper but a sharp weakened point must be avoided (figure 22). For the grooved setting already mentioned, the narrow end should be rounded over and have sufficient thickness to provide a clearance for the saw blade. Draw the chosen shape on the trimmed blank with an aluminium marker, either freehand or using a template. Pre-forming with a trim saw will remove some of the unwanted material.

Using a 120 or 100 grit wheel, grind to the perimeter outline keeping the sides level and at right angles to the faces of the stone. At this stage do not attempt to round off the domed portions as this may lead to over-cutting on one side and loss of symmetry. Dop the stone on a stick using wax or one of the other dopping methods referred to previously. With an aluminium marker scribe a line round the stone at the halfway point, dividing the depth into two equal parts. As an aid a thin strip of waterproof adhesive tape can be stuck round the stone with a straight edge on the marked line (figure 23). During the grinding the tape should remain in position long enough to establish the girdle and limits of the first dome. The tape will prevent any tendency to cut below the original line and will also lessen the risk of chipping or flaking below the line that sometimes occurs with brittle stones. As usual, water coolant is used throughout all stages of grinding and sanding.

Start cutting the first cabochon side, still using the 100

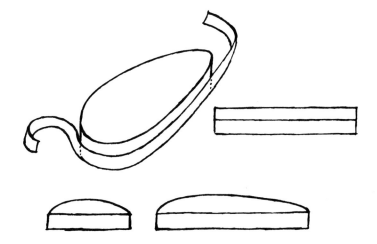

Fig 23 Half depth marked by pencil line or adhesive strip to cut first dome of double cabochon.

or 120 grinding wheel, with a series of bevels that are steeper at the broad end and shallower towards the narrow end. Cut successive stepped bevels in this way, gradually working towards the centre and repeatedly checking the end and side profiles until a rough basic shape is achieved (figure 24). A straight edge that is parallel to, but not touching, the masking tape should be formed around the dome to allow for a slight spread during further grinding and sanding. The golden rule applicable to every type of cabochon is *never attempt to grind the dome from the centre towards the outer edge of a stone*, always work from the edge inwards to retain full height in the dome. Final shaping will remove all points and flat places and at this stage the stone must be constantly moving against the grinding wheel using moderate pressure. With elongated stones such as pendants it is essential to have the wheel trued to a level grinding face as sharp flanges on a grooved wheel will restrict freedom of manipulation.

Repeat the smoothing actions on a 220 grinding wheel, using light pressure and continuous movements, turning the dopstick. Carry out sanding, or refinement of the surface, in the usual manner on a 220 grit wet/dry disc followed by a 400 grit disc. At this stage the stone should

Fig 24 Angles of stepped bevels during shaping.

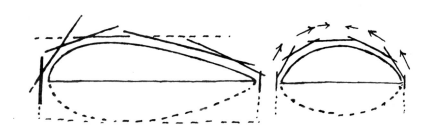

begin to show a slight polish but, if desired, sanding can be continued on a finer 600 grit disc.

Normally, with a single cabochon, final polishing would take place at this point, but for the present project polishing is delayed until the reverse cabochon has been cut and sanded. The reasons for suggesting this are that dopping wax does not adhere so well to a polished surface, and additionally, some minor adjustments to the shape of the first dome may become necessary to produce matching curves.

Peel off the adhesive strip if it is still in position and remove the stone from the dopstick. Do not re-dop on the reverse side at this stage.

The problem of matching the curves in the two halves now arises if a symmetrical shape is desired, and this is best achieved by preliminary shaping and roughing out of the second cabochon with the stone off the dopstick so that checks can be made from all angles. Cut down to the girdle or halfway line and establish a parallel edge. The girdle can be finished off as a narrow flat band or rounded over.

It is now possible to continue the entire process by manipulating the stone in the fingers, but some will find it more convenient to re-dop for the fine grinding and sanding stages. In fact, many cutters have sufficient skill and confidence to cut a double cabochon without using a dopstick at all.

When the pendant is an evenly balanced shape, complete the fine grinding on a 220 wheel followed by the same sanding stages as before and then continue through final polishing with one of the oxide slurries. Remove from the dopstick and polish the other half of the stone, paying particular attention to the girdle area, and establish an even gloss over the whole surface.

The Grooved Setting

The type of pendant setting made with silver wire let into a continuous groove round the stone, shown in figure 25, is made possible by using a trim saw to cut a fine depression into the girdle. This sawing must be done before the stone is finally polished to prevent the blade skidding off course and preferably where the girdle has been left as a narrow flat band.

Hold the stone firmly between the finger tips of both hands and rotate it slowly against the revolving saw blade until a groove is cut round the perimeter (figure 26). This action should be practised on an alternative piece of stone to establish the correct degree of control. When the

Fig 25 Double cabochons. Pendant at bottom left shows wire setting in continuous groove.

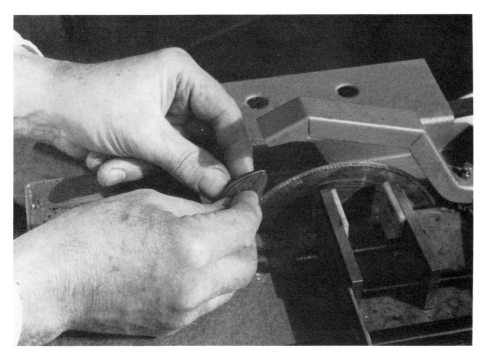

groove is cut, sand the girdle once more to smooth out any irregularities and then polish as usual.

Fig 26 Sawing a groove in pendant rim.

SQUARE CUSHION SHAPE

Allow sufficient depth of stone for the raised crown in this case and trim on the saw to a square perimeter. The four sides and base can be trued up on a flat lap and a very fine bevel cut round the base edges to remove sharpness and prevent chipping.

The upper domed portion of the stone can be formed in different ways (figure 27). For example, the dome can sweep down to the base edge in one continuous movement, or it can be interrupted by a line parallel to the base to give a girdle thickness which is varied in depth as desired. Alternatively, the curvature of the dome can spring from each of the four sides, producing ribbed junctions leading down to the corners. These ridges can either be retained as a feature or made less pronounced by careful grinding. Alternatively they could be smoothed away entirely.

If girdle walls are to be left, decide on their depth and draw a line with an aluminium scriber each side parallel to the base edge and accurately joined at the four corners. The stone can be dopped at this stage for ease of handling.

To shape the curved crown grind on the front face of a level 100 or 120 grinding wheel, start by cutting a bevel

Fig 27 Cushion shape variations.

41

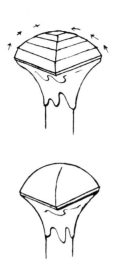

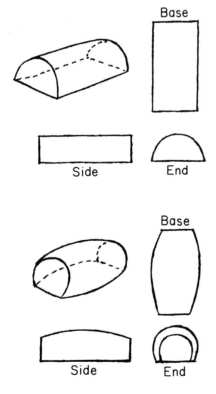

Fig 28 Shaping the curved crown.

Fig 29 Alternative barrel shapes.

on each of the four sides at approximately 45 degrees to line up horizontally on the aluminium mark. Do not over-cut the line or the symmetry will be lost, bear in mind that further refinement stages will remove additional material. If girdle walls are not required the 45 degree bevel can be taken almost to the base. Continue cutting bevels upwards towards the centre of the dome, lessening the angles progressively towards the top and finally rounding off the faces in sweeping curves from base to top. This will produce four curved faces meeting at the ridges which terminate in a point (figure 28).

The height of the crown may be cut to any desired depth for either a steep or shallow profile and the four ridges can be rounded over or eliminated near the top of the dome to give a smooth curved surface. The cut may be further varied by sloping the girdle walls inwards instead of being vertical and this is done prior to cutting the domed portion. Complete the shaping on a finer grinding wheel and carry out the usual sanding and polishing stages.

BARREL SHAPES

Barrel shapes are based on forms resembling half a barrel cut in longitudinal section with the two ends flat and vertical. The base can be rectangular or slightly curved at the sides, and the domed profile can be level at the top or suggest downward curvature at both ends (figure 29). Stones cut in this style are ideally suited for use as cuff-links.

Select a thick slab, about 1 cm ($\frac{1}{2}$ in), to allow a margin for errors and trimmed with a flat face on both top and bottom. If a banded material is chosen the straight lines can be orientated to run the length of the stone to serve as a guide to symmetry during cutting. The width and length of the piece of stone will depend on the planned proportion of the base.

Draw the base shape, either rectangular or curved, directly on the stone with an aluminium scriber. Plastic and metal templates usually offer several rectangular shapes of different proportions but if a curved base is preferred this can be pre-planned and a template cut from adhesive material to stick on the stone.

Cut the base shape on a coarse grinding wheel to the aluminium line or edge of the adhesive template shape which can then be peeled off. Grind the usual fine bevel on the base perimeter to clean up the shape and reinforce the edge. At this point the stone is dopped.

Start shaping the upper domed portion by cutting

steep bevels on the two long sides and continue in a
series of further stepped bevels towards the top of the
stone in decreasing angles. In the case of a curved shape
the bevels should sweep from right to left in a gradual
curve (figure 30).

The next stage is to remove the stepped ridges formed
by the overlapping bevels.

Still using the coarse wheel, which should have a level
face and not be grooved, position the stone so that the
ridges are horizontal across the face of the wheel. By
careful manipulation of the dopstick roll the stone
upwards and downwards against the wheel in a continuous rocking movement that will smooth the dome down
to the base. With a curved perimeter, use a similar action
but at the same time curve gently from left to right. This
combined action will need practice and repeated progress
checks are necessary to ensure an evenly balanced profile. Continue until all the ridges have been removed and
the curved barrel shape has been formed to satisfaction.

To check the overall shape hold the dopstick upright
with the stone at eye level, preferably against a light back-
ground. With the curved barrel top, the profile should
show a gentle curve higher in the centre sloping down
towards the ends. Slowly tilt the dopstick backward then
forward so that any changes in the curved outline will
immediately be apparent. If bumps, flats or any other
irregularities are present the faults must be corrected
before going on with the refining stages on the 220 grit
wheel. The usual sequences of sanding are carried out on
220 and 400 grit discs, drum or belt sander.

The two vertical ends of the barrel should be cut and
sanded before polishing the dome and it may be found
more convenient to remove the stone from the dopstick
and control it in the fingers, particularly when using a
flat lap or during sanding. It will also be easier to judge
whether the ends are forming at right angles to the base.
When each stage has been completed the whole stone
can be finally polished. Cutting a second barrel shape to
form a matching pair for cuff-links will be the real test of
skill.

HEART SHAPES

This popular gemstone shape can be reproduced in
many sizes and used as single stones for pendants or in
multiples for bracelets. The heart shape can be cut either
with a single dome and flat back or as a double-sided
cabochon but in the latter case the trimmed slab will
need a greater thickness (figure 31). Plastic templates

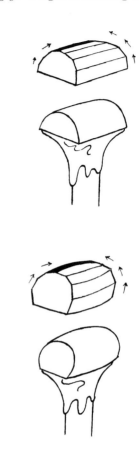

Fig 30 Stages in forming barrel

Fig 31 Allow double thickness for double cabochon heart shape.

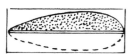

offer a limited choice of heart shapes in two or three sizes but if these do not meet requirements there is a quick method of drawing a presentable shape for direct transfer to the trimmed stone or to make an adhesive template. A few practice drawings will help decide the most suitable size and all that is needed is a piece of plain paper, pencil and a few different sizes of flat buttons or small coins. Drawing instruments could be used but are not really necessary.

Rule a few centre guidelines in different parts of the paper and select buttons or coins to provide alternative proportions, then proceed as illustrated in figure 32, With a little practice it is easy to draw a well-proportioned shape which can be elongated or compressed according to taste. The chosen heart shape can then be cut out with scissors and used as a guide for marking on the stone. If the shape is cut from a piece of contact adhesive material it can be stuck on the stone and allowed to remain in position until the grinding of the basic outline is completed.

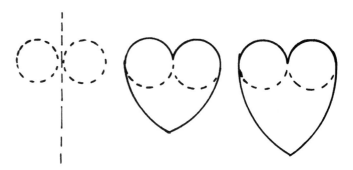

Fig 32 Planning a heart shape.

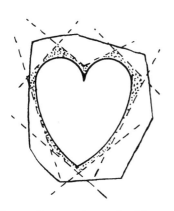

Fig 33 Stone trimmed with saw (dotted lines).

Some of the superfluous portions of the stone can be removed with a trim saw to save grinding (figure 33). When sawing into the 'V' shape at the top of the heart remember to stop well short of the line as the curvature of the saw blade will cut further into the underneath part of the stone which is not visible. If the cut reaches the line or template edge on the upper surface it will have cut too far on the underside.

With medium to hard stones (Mohs' 6 and above) grinding can start on a 120 grit wheel, but for softer or brittle stones a 220 grit wheel is preferable. Remove sharp corners and establish the required shape but retain flat surfaces of the slab at front and rear until basic shaping is completed. The outline of the lower curves and pointed end of the heart can be cut without difficulty on the front face of a level wheel but the 'V' shaped top will require extra care, making use of the corner or edge of the wheel as shown in the accompanying diagrams (figure 34).

In the case of a single cabochon, when the basic shape has been cut, a small bevel is ground on the edge of the flat base to prevent chipping. With a double cabochon, draw a line round the stone to half the depth and cut the first dome to this girdle line. With regard to dopping, it is preferable not to use a dopstick as this will restrict movement and delicacy of handling while shaping difficult areas. Holding the stone in the fingers will give more sensitive contact with the wheel and the worked portions can be freely observed at all times. If the proportions of the heart shape are too small to hold it comfortably then it should be dopped, but only on a short dopstick leaving just enough room for the fingers to be in contact with the stick or wax allowing closer control.

Preliminary cutting of the domed portion should establish an even bevel on the outer edge of the stone almost down to the base or the halfway mark of a double cabochon. Retain the height of the central part of the dome as long as possible, bearing in mind the useful rule of always shaping the dome from the outer edge inwards and never the other way round. When bevelling the 'V'-shaped area the angle of the stone must be tilted to cut each side of the centre point against left and right corners of the grinding wheel (figures 36–38). The bevel angles on the upper part of the stone should be steeper than those cut towards the pointed end. By changing angles of cut, gradually work inwards in a series of steps until the centre is reached. There should be a greater fullness, or height of contour, nearer the top half of the heart, while the shallower angles cut lower down the stone should result in a gentle taper towards the point (figure 35).

To achieve a good profile shape the stone must be inspected frequently at eye level, both from side and end, to assess the symmetry since this is such an important factor in a heart-shaped stone. The technique of working the 'V' shape is vital; one half overhanging the corner and projecting down the side but not touching the wheel. This, of course, refers to vertical grinding wheels and anyone who is cutting on a horizontal wheel can easily adapt to a comparable method.

Final shaping and removal of points and ridges should be done on a 120 wheel in the case of hard stones and surface refinements completed on a 220 wheel before moving on to the sanding stages. Sanding the stone

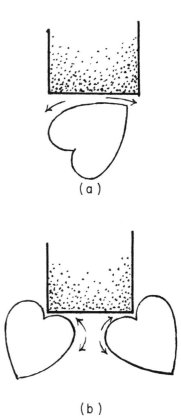

Fig 34 (a) Outline shape cut on front edge. (b) V shape cut on corners of the wheel.

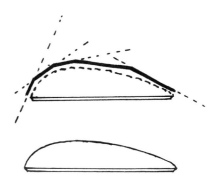

Fig 35 Series of bevels to give fullness of height and gradual taper.

Fig 36 Position of stone to shape left lobe of the heart.

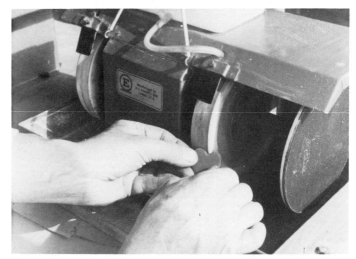

Fig 37 Cutting the right lobe.

Fig 38 Shaping towards the point of the domed heart.

successively on 220 and 400 wet/dry discs will follow similar patterns of movement with the top curves of the heart never on the disc at the same time, thus preventing a flat plane forming. Each lobe should be smoothed in a rounding, downwards motion while the other half overhangs the edge of the disc; gradually sand towards the the centre and into the lower pointed half (figure 39).

Polishing will present fewer problems since the danger of cutting into the stone accidentally or adding unwanted facets will not arise. The corner of a felt polishing pad can be worked into the 'V' shape as the stone is manipulated in this awkward area.

With the double-sided heart shape the aim should be perfect symmetry from every angle and an unwavering girdle between the two halves. If the stone has been dopped to cut the first side it is advisable to cut the second half off the dop in order to be able to assess the shaping process and compare profiles of both sides.

Several methods of mounting the finished stone are possible but in every case the heart shape should not be obscured by the fitting. For this reason drilling a neat hole in the V and inserting a pegged ring for a chain attachment is possibly the most suitable solution (figures 40 and 41).

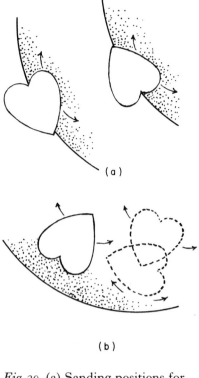

(a)

(b)

Fig 39 (a) Sanding positions for domed lobes. (b) Varying positions for other parts of dome – arrows indicate direction of rocking movement.

Fig 40 Examples of heart shapes. *Left :* silver wire loop inserted in drilled hole for a pendant hanging.

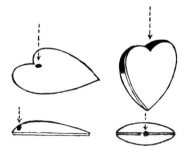

Fig 41 Alternative placing of the drilled holes.

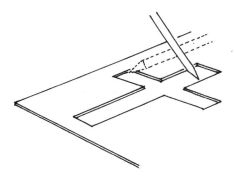

Fig 42 Hold sharpened point at angle against template.

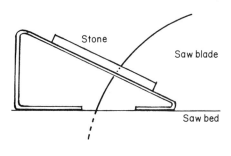

Fig 43 Angled metal support as sawing aid.

CROSSES

Cutting a cross successfully starts at the slabbing stage with a smoothly cut parallel slice of rock, followed by meticulously accurate sawing on a trim saw to arrive at a finished shape almost at once. If the saw cuts are true, giving smooth clean faces, further shaping will be minimized. The portions likely to give trouble are the four corners created at the intersection of the vertical and horizontal arms of the cross. A great deal can be accomplished by a sawing technique designed to offset the curvature of the saw blade and a well-dressed or new grinding wheel with right-angled side and front faces will give greater precision when sharpening up the corner sections.

Choose a smooth slab of reasonable thickness and trim off a rectangle to contain the required cruciform shape. The arms of the cross can be equal in width and depth which is, of course, determined by the thickness of the slab. It is possible to cut crosses from thinner slabs with the depth only half the width of the arms but remember that projections are vulnerable to knocks, and stones that are brittle should not be used, nor should those with pronounced cleavage or lamillar planes.

Where a template is being used, mark out the position of the cross by scribing the line close to the template opening. Sharpen the aluminium marker to a fine point and hold it at an angle when drawing to retain maximum outline of the cross shape and ensure good delineation of the corners (figure 42). When drawing a cross without the aid of a template be sure to scribe parallel widths and place the horizontal members precisely at right-angles to the vertical.

The sawing aid shown in figure 43 will position the slab at a convenient angle to the trim saw blade and lessen risks of over-cutting by the curving blade. For precision cutting of this nature it is absolutely essential to have a clean coolant tank and fresh cutting oil. Dirty oil and churned up sludge will quickly obscure the marked oulines of the cross when cutting starts and make the task impossible. Clean oil is transparent and as the stone is on a slope the oil will not accumulate but will run slowly down to the base of the saw, leaving the silvery lines of the marked cross clearly defined. Saw carefully on the outside of the scribed lines, easing off the pressure as the blade approaches intersecting lines and drawing the stone back sharply at the right-angled junction of the two cuts as they meet and the stone breaks away. All cuts running in the same direction must be parallel to ensure

1.   A selection of agates showing the wide range of patterns and colours

2. Cabochons. *Left to right*
    1st row: Petrified wood, blue tiger's-eye, golden tiger's eye, blue lace
              agate, Iona marble
    2nd row: Green aventurine, thulite, petrified wood, malachite, rhyolite
    3rd row: Amethyst, amozonite, moss opal, blue aventurine, hickoryite
    4th row: Dumortierite, rhodochrosite, petrified wood, grossular garnet,
              agate
    5th row: Carnelian, agate, red aventurine, Indian jasper, crazy lace agate

even dimensions across the width of the arms. Any widening or narrowing towards the ends or centre will impose additional grinding and lapping problems, in fact it may even result in altering the width of each arm in turn to obtain uniform measurements. One of the worst sawing faults likely to occur is bad alignment of the saw cut at each side of the intersection (figure 44) and in this case much frustrating grinding will be necessary to correct the error.

If the stone has snapped away at the junction of the saw cuts the centre angles will need sharpening up and possibly a projecting nub may have to be ground away. For this, and any other further shaping or removal of saw cuts, a new or freshly dressed grinding wheel is imperative. One of the projecting arms of the cross will lay along the front face and the other at right angles down the side of the wheel. Before the wheel is set in motion place the cross in each required position to both left and right sides of the wheel. Inspect closely from above and check whether any gaps are present between wheel and stone at the front and side, also see that the corner of the wheel fits snugly into the angled junctions (figure 45). If gaps are evident this will indicate the extent of additional shaping needed, always assuming that the wheel face is true and at right angles.

During grinding hold the stone firmly in the correct position to the wheel to retain flat faces. There is a strong tendency for the cross to twist in the fingers and this must be avoided otherwise a series of unwanted facets will be produced. Keep a close check also on the corner of the grinding wheel to make sure it does not gouge into one of the arms. Small bevels can be added along the lengths of each sharp edge to prevent chipping.

If the cutting stages just described are being carried out on a flat lap with loose grits the same advice will hold good. The lap surface must be level, if not it should be milled until smooth. The worked surface of the stone will lay in a horizontal position along the lap with the right-angled projection pointing downwards over the edge of the lap. The task will be easier if the lapping plate has a generous depth to guide the overhanging portion of the cross. The grit sequences for both grinding wheels and loose abrasives will depend on the amount of work to be done at this point to get the cross to a true shape but it is hoped that few adjustments will be necessary (figures 46, 47 and 48).

When the cross has been squared up to satisfaction it is a good time to drill a hole either completely through for a

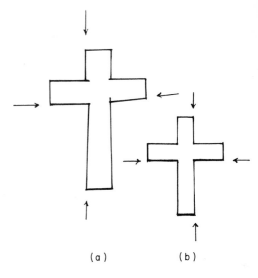

Fig 44 (a) Bad alignment of saw cuts. (b) Correctly sawn.

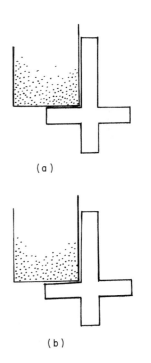

Fig 45 Testing right-angled faces. (a) Matching right-angles. (b) Gaps show angles out of true.

49

Fig 46 Cutting a square-sectioned cross.

Fig 47 Sanding a square-sectioned cross.

Fig 48 Shaping a square-sectioned cross on a flat lap.

jump ring or at the top for a pegged hanging (figure 49). It is better to drill the stone before sanding and polishing as the drill tip tends to skid on a fine smooth surface.

The sanding stages can be done on wet/dry sanding discs in either horizontal or vertical positions, or continued on a flat lap with finer abrasives. Sanding discs that are slightly larger than the backing pads can present sharp cutting edges and there is some danger of grooving the overhanging portions of the cross if care is not exercised. The sequence is to complete the eight sides in rotation on the 220 grit disc, then the four ends. Do not forget to sand the bevels on the corners or angled edges, holding the cross in the most convenient positions. Finally, concentrate on the front and rear main faces. It is important to follow an ordered pattern of sanding otherwise one of the sides or edges might be omitted. Repeat the entire sequence on a 400 grit disc or use 400 to 600 grit slurries on a metal lap until each surface is satin smooth. At all stages care must be taken to hold the face being worked perfectly flat against the abrasive surface.

Before going on to the polishing stage clean the stone thoroughly, taking particular care to rinse any grit from drilled holes, then dry and inspect under a good light. It may be found that the corners at the angled junctions are not completely sanded and in this case silicon carbide sticks can be rubbed by hand into these difficult areas. Alternatively a piece of wet/dry paper wrapped round an angular stick will serve the same purpose (figure 50).

Polish in the usual manner on a vertical or horizontal polishing pad, again allowing one arm of the cross to overhang the side while polishing the right-angled face.

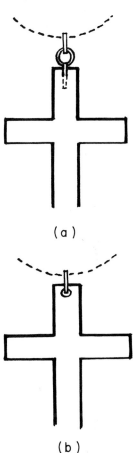

Fig 49 Alternative drilling positions for support (a) from above, (b) from front.

(a)

(b)

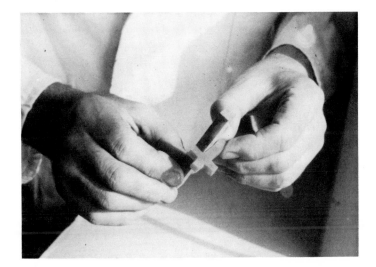

Fig 50 Sharpening up corners with silicon carbide stick.

51

By increasing pressure on the corner of the felt lap it is possible to force the polish into the more awkward recesses of the cross shape. Make sure that every side and bevel is polished in turn and that none is overlooked.

Variations on the Cross Shape

Following the successful completion of a cross by the methods described, several alternative styles may be introduced. One of the simplest of these is a cross with half-round or entirely circular bars (figures 51, 52). After pre-forming on a trim saw to give angular square-sectioned faces the cross bars are then rounded on the front face of a level grinding wheel.

The technique for cutting a cross with cylindrical upright and cross members is as follows: place the arm to be shaped across the front face of the grinding wheel with the right-angled arm down the side but not touching the wheel; slowly turn the stone in the fingers of both hands to grind an evenly rounded form (figures 53, 54).; cut all four projecting arms of the cross in this way, leaving a small square projecting tablet in the centre; sand and polish to complete. As a further variation a cabochon of appropriate size could be cut in a contrasting stone and then glued in position on the raised square.

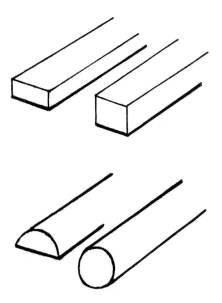

Fig 51 Alternative sections.

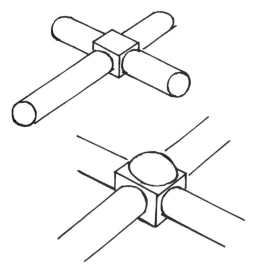

Fig 52 Round section with raised centre square.

Fig 53 Cutting a round section cross. Turn slowly in fingers of right hand, support with finger of left hand.

Fig 54 Sanding round sectioned cross.

Fig 55 Cross shapes. *Centre* – method of support using upeye fitting cemented to the top.

GEOMETRIC CUTS

The term *geometric cuts* is not an accepted classification of known styles but it is used here to describe a few selected shapes that fall into an ordered category, and also to distinguish them from cabochons and other cuts previously mentioned. Stones falling under this heading include those cut into a variety of geometric shapes having regular perimeter outlines in the case of flat stones and symmetry of form around a central axis in drop or pendant shapes.

Cutting Flat Stones

These are intended for ring or cuff-link settings or in any circumstances where a bezel setting is employed to secure stones with regular outlines such as ovals, circles, squares or rectangles. Such stones are very shallow in section and apart from a fine setting bevel round the edge are finished entirely flat with little or no projection above the bezel rim when set (figure 56). Stones cut in this way have long been fashionable for men's rings, cuff-links and tie-tacks, and are frequently cut from varieties of chalcedony for strength and durability. Black or banded black and white onyx, sard, carnelian and bloodstone are popular for the smaller stones, while the banding and pictorial patterns in colourful jaspers and agates are more fully exploited as larger stones set in brooches. Apart from cutting to modern requirements and standard template shapes, many items of antique jewellery are available in which a damaged stone needs replacing. In such cases it is advisable to retain the original stone if possible in order to match the size and shape of cut to fit the setting.

Select a suitable piece of stone and saw into thin section. The thickness will depend upon the setting requirements, for example whether the flat top of the stone will correspond with the bezel height or be slightly raised. Make allowance also for the amount of cutting that may be needed to level or lower the flat surface and the subsequent sanding stages. Mark out the shape and trim close to the planned outline of a square or rectangular stone with the saw. In the case of round or oval stones trim off unwanted material to reduce the amount of subsequent grinding. Establish the exact perimeter shape by careful grinding on the wheel or square up the straight sides of angular stones on a flat metal lap with loose grits. If the original trimming allowed extra thickness for removal of saw marks, the visible face should be sanded down on a flat lap until perfectly level by using

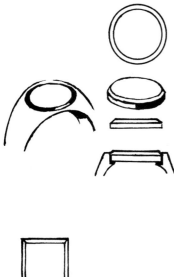

Fig 56 Flat stones with narrow bevels. Round and square shapes associated with settings.

54

220 grit, followed by refinements with finer grades. Where the stone is small and almost wafer thin it may be difficult to control with the fingers alone and dopping will be necessary. If preferred, the smooth level surface can be taken through the final sanding stages on rigidly supported sanding discs or belts – resilient cushioned drum sanders will tend to round over the edges and miss the centre part of the stone.

Complete the shaping by cutting a bevel on the rim of the upper surface. With circular and elliptical stones, cut the bevel on a fine grinding wheel using a sweeping action, keeping the angle constant throughout and maintaining a controlled turning movement with the dopstick. In a similar way it is possible to cut fine bevels using the flat surface of end sanders. Constant checks are necessary to ensure that an even bevel of equal depth is being formed round the stone since any error becomes very obvious when aligned against the edge of a bezel setting. It is also important not to allow the bevels to overcut the base of the stone or form a razor-sharp girdle edge that is liable to crumble as the metal is pressed over the stone during setting.

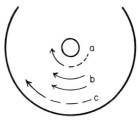

a. Slower surface rotation
b. Intermediary speeds
c. Faster surface rotation

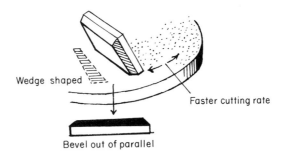

Wedge shaped

Faster cutting rate

Bevel out of parallel

Four-sided stones can be bevelled by holding at the correct angle on the lap and it is important that the bevels work out parallel on all sides to meet evenly at the corners (figure 57). With slightly thicker angular stones the bevels can be cut first, then the upper surface can be cut in a perfectly horizontal plane to the required depth. In this way the bevels will be level and the corners in alignment. Care must be taken in the sanding stages not to destroy the straight edges of the bevels.

Polish the stones in the usual way, starting with the bevels and completing the large upper face. A firm polishing lap will help retain a sharp ridge between the flat face and the bevelled edges. In many cases it will only be necessary to polish the upper surface of the stone as the underside will not be visible in the setting.

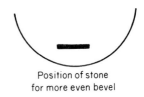

Position of stone
for more even bevel

Fig 57 Position of stone for cutting parallel bevels using flat lap.

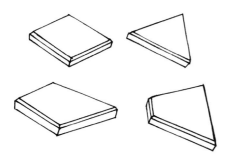

Fig 58 Flat variations

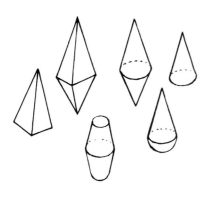

Fig 59 Geometric cuts in the round.

Other Flat Variations

Stones conforming to a symmetrical geometry of outline such as triangular, lozenge, trapezoid and kite shapes, as shown in figure 58, can be cut for specific jewellery purposes and set in a number of ways. These include larger pendants with bezel settings or simply attached to bell caps, or the stone can be drilled through to take a jump ring. A wider choice of gemstone material can be introduced to include some of the softer stones and greater emphasis placed on special features such as pattern and colour.

Cutting and polishing procedures are as previously described: starting with trimming to the basic outline with the saw, followed by squaring up the shape and bevelling both upper and lower edges. If the bevels are cut to deeper proportions as a decorative feature a polished reflective band will echo the outline shape. Both sides of the stone should be polished so that either side can be worn uppermost when it is freely suspended in an open setting.

Geometric Cuts in the Round

Designs similar to those illustrated in figure 59 will encompass a variety of lapidary skills using saw, flat lap, grinders and the appropriate range of finishing processes. One of the requirements here is total symmetry around a central axis and, whatever shape is chosen, the finished stone should hang evenly when secured at the tapered apex. Stones cut in this way will be suitable for pendant drops or, on a smaller scale, for earrings and bracelet hangings.

Circular Cone Drop

Start by cutting the stone into a cylindrical shape which can be tested for uniformity by passing it through a template of the required diameter. Form the cylinder on the front edge of a level grinding wheel, turning the stone in the fingers and carrying out regular checks along the total length with the template. When the cylindrical pre-form is completed a small spot can be marked in the centre of the circular top to help in centring the tip of the cone. Continue cutting in a similar way but holding the stone at suitable angles to shape a cone, gradually tapering from the top and retaining the full circular girdle width at the base. Make sure that the pointed apex is in a central position (figure 60).

There are several ways of treating the base or wider part of the drop. If it is to be left entirely flat a small

56

bevel must be cut on the circular edge to prevent chipping. Alternatively the base can be rounded in a shallow curve or shaped in a full hemispherical cabochon. In such cases a girdle line will be formed and this must be kept level and as straight as possible round the circumference.

Shaping is followed by sanding and polishing carried out in the usual way. Some type of bell cap fastenings will be required to secure stones on the selected fittings such as earrings, bracelet or pendant chain.

Square Based Pyramid

This shape is for devotees of the flat lap and demands careful judgment to attain uniformity in the four tapering faces. The drop can be cut as a single pyramid with a flat base slightly bevelled on the edges, or a double form with tapering sides above and below a central girdle. A sequence for cutting is illustrated in figure 61.

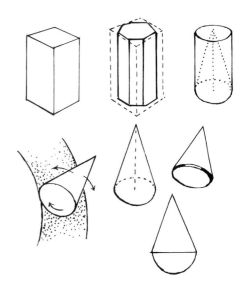

Fig 60 Development of the cone shape.

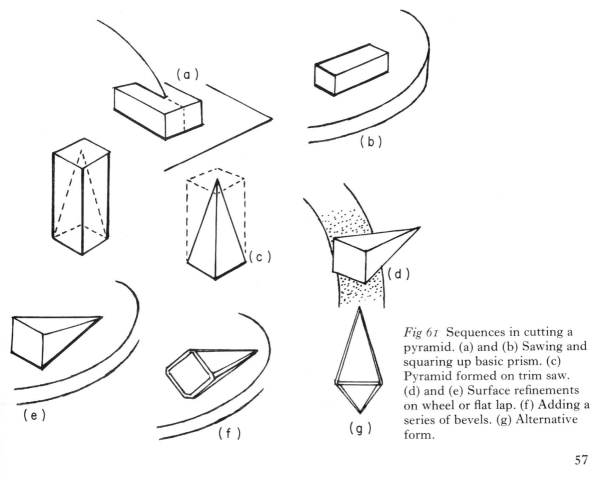

Fig 61 Sequences in cutting a pyramid. (a) and (b) Sawing and squaring up basic prism. (c) Pyramid formed on trim saw. (d) and (e) Surface refinements on wheel or flat lap. (f) Adding a series of bevels. (g) Alternative form.

57

The logical starting shape is an elongated square prism that is long enough to contain the proposed drop shape. Cut to shape on the trim saw and sand the ends and four longer faces on the lap. For the tapering faces, decide which is to be the base of the pyramid and from a point at the apex draw a triangle on each side with an aluminium scriber. Pre-form on the front edge of a grinding wheel or with the trim saw if the scale of the work makes this possible. Cut on the outside of the scribed lines to make allowance for subsequent removal of material at lapping stages.

Lap each of the flat faces in rotation, a little at a time to retain the symmetry, until they meet at a central point and form sharp ridges down the length. If excessive stock removal is necessary begin with coarse abrasives, 80 or 100 grit, on the flat lap. Continue through the refinement stages sanding with grades from 220 through to 500 grit. Sanding is also possible on rigid sanding discs of similar grades. In the absence of a flat lapping machine each stage can be carried out on plate glass and acrylic sheet with loose grit slurries.

Polishing the flat faces is done on a firm lapping surface to retain maximum sharpness of the ridges and scored acrylic discs or firm leather laps are preferable to felt for this purpose. Many variations of shape and further embellishments are shown in figure 69.

Fig 62 Stones cut with balanced symmetry. *Top row :* varied outline shapes, flat sections front and rear. *Bottom row : centre –* two cushion shapes, *right –* barrel shape.

LAPPING HINTS

Horizontal laps, preferably of cast iron, provide a good base for loose grit slurries when cutting flat faces and bevels on stones (figures 63, 64). The metal laps are subjected to the same abrasive action as the stones and over a prolonged period of use a slight hollow will be worn between the outer rim and centre of the lap. This usually occurs at the most effective cutting area, since this is the part most often used when lapping small stones. This accounts for problems where abrasion seems less pronounced in the centre of the stones than at the edges. Where this occurs the lap should be milled flat at the earliest opportunity.

Fig 63 Evans 20 cm (8 in) horizontal metal lap with interchangeable polishing disc. *H.C. Evans & Sons, Sidcup, England.*

Fig 64 Gemtek flat lap with continuous metal lap surface and separate polishing disc. *Gemstones Ltd, Hull, England.*

Using a wider area of the lap by traversing the stone across the disc will help to maintain a level surface, but leading and trailing edges of the stone will have to be reversed periodically to counteract different rates of cutting. When holding a stone on a lap there is a tendency to apply a little more pressure on the edge leading head-on to the turning lap in order to prevent the stone spinning off. This often leads to uneven cutting and a series of shallow facets on the surface, particularly if any slight rocking of the stone takes place and contact with the lap is subjected to fluctuating pressures (figures 65, 66). It should also be remembered that abrasion is more rapid towards the periphery of the lap owing to increased surface speeds.

Fig 65 Facets occurring on flat surface of the stone due to rocking and uneven pressures.

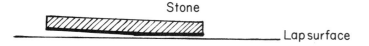

Stone

Lap surface

Fig 66 Holding stone in flat contact with lap, using both hands to prevent rocking.

To cut bevels and tapering faces on the geometric cuts requires a little care. The bevels need to be formed at the same angles to avoid a series of step cuts, so once the stone has been placed in contact with the lap it must remain in a fixed position. In order that the bevel runs in a parallel band and is not splayed out towards one end, the stone should be held in a position as shown in figure 57.

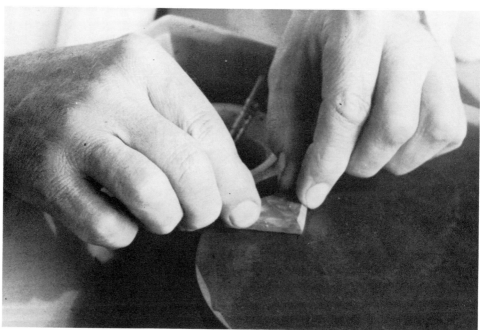

Fig 67 Cinch setting with interchangeable polished agates. Circular outline, polished both sides with fine bevels cut on perimeter.

Fig 68 Necklace and matching earrings of Brazilian agate. Triangular shapes lapped and polished in thin sections.

FREE-FORMS

Within this category the term *cabochet* is now widely used to denote gem cuts which incorporate the domed shapes of cabochons with flat or faceted portions. These are freely formed on grinding wheels and flat lap without the mechanical aid of a faceting head. Cabochets are recognized as a competition class at gem shows and are defined for judging purposes as 'regular or irregular shaped stones combining flat and curved faces arranged in any manner' (figure 69).

The appeal of cabochets worked as creative exercises is that the cutter is not bound by restrictions of styles, sizes or types of gem material, but far from being a haphazard affair all the skills of cutting and polishing are present. When cut and finished to perfection and mounted as jewellery this type of stone is singularly attractive.

Due to the fact that in many instances free-forms are the outcome of accidental and purely intuitive changes of shape during cutting, it is only possible to introduce a general approach to this kind of creative cutting, supported by worked examples. Many lapidaries will find this a satisfying and complete break from the more formal disciplines of faceting and the endless similarities of calibrated cabochons.

A starting point may be suggested by an irregular chunky piece of gemstone rough which has been hammered from a larger lump. On close examination a number of rough planes in opposing directions may be present and these could be tentatively levelled on the grinding wheel, leading finally to flattened facets using the flat lap. Other parts of the stone may have pronounced convex curves which form obvious cabochon features and these should be exploited on the wheel. Develop both the flats and curves gradually, working them in conjunction with each other and avoiding the temptation to complete any one face to the exclusion of others. In this way shaping is controlled and a general design unity will be retained. Throughout all the initial stages of cutting the aim should be for a stone of pleasing proportions.

Features in the stone, such as shallow cracks and pits, that require special attention to grind level can be the start of a new facet. The accidental changes mentioned earlier can occur during grinding where, for example, a piece of stone flakes off and the resulting uneven fracture has to be ground away, producing a change of angle and a further facet.

If desired the overall design of a cabochet can be pre-

Fig 69 Top rows – assortment of free forms. *Third row* – cabochets. *Fourth row* – geometric drops in the round.

determined and sketches prepared to show a rough idea of side and front elevations. If such sketches are made they should be regarded only as a starting point and should be subject to modifications during the more creative act of cutting. Cabochets are often easier to handle during shaping when designed as pendants, since the extra size allows greater scope for changes of surface. Where a cabochet is designed more formally, with a central cabochon dome surrounded by a series of regular or irregular facets, it will be necessary to shape the curved portion first and then place the facets in position. The edges where flat faces meet should be straight and clear cut so a firmer polishing lap is preferable to prevent rounding over of sharp ridges. Hard leather is better than the more resilient felt lap; alternatively borrow the facetor's method of using a scored acrylic lap charged with polishing oxide.

Many interesting experiments can be carried out on different types of gem rough, exploiting either the properties of transparent quartz varieties or the colour and reflective surfaces of opaque materials. Contrast can be introduced by deliberately leaving some facets unpolished to emphasize the brilliance of completed neighbouring facets. The resulting cabochets will present many challenging problems for those who design and make their own jewellery settings but the finished effect will be an entirely individual and original creation.

COMPOSITE STONES

By utilizing different types of gem rough to make up composite or laminated stones, added interest can be given to cabochons and other cuts already described. During selection and cutting much will be learned about the optical features and advantageous orientation of the materials used.

Selected stones must be of similar hardness to avoid problems of undercutting which occur in material with hard and soft portions – probably the most frequent cause of irregularities of finish. To cut single cabochons with two or more laminated layers of stone the rough must be trimmed to very thin slices to control the overall thickness. In the case of a composite block to be slabbed and trimmed in different ways, thicker pieces of stone can be stuck together. The faces of the stones to be joined must be sanded absolutely flat to make perfect contact. If this is not done efficiently minute cavities will appear at the edges of the laminations during shaping.

Cement the layers with a hard setting, clear, water-

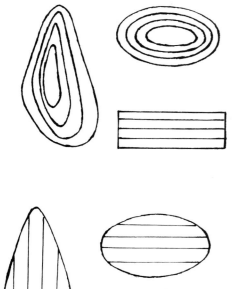

Fig 70 Alternative banding arrangement of composite layers.

64

proof adhesive applied in a thin film to each adjoining face. Slide the stones together rather than placing one on the other as this will eliminate air pockets. Wipe surplus adhesive from the edges of the joints and allow to set thoroughly before beginning cutting.

The direction in which the laminated blocks are slabbed will determine the arrangement of consecutive banding formed by the different coloured layers, giving either parallel stripes along the length of the stone or formation of a series of concentric rings in a domed cabochon. The banding can be placed symmetrically or form an off-centred contour pattern in irregular or free-form shapes (figure 70). Once the blanks have been prepared and orientated in such a way as to supply the desired effects, cutting and polishing should proceed in the usual way. Added interest can be achieved by incorporating silver and copper strips into the laminations, always bearing in mind comparative hardnesses. In the polishing stages it will be found that any such metal inclusions will darken the lap and discolour the polishing oxides, but this is not detrimental.

Other variations are accomplished by sawing up strongly patterned stone and re-assembling the pieces in different formations. A good example to illustrate the effectiveness of this is the popular chatoyant quartz gemstone, golden tiger's eye. As the bands of light are formed at right-angles to the fibrous structure the material can be cut and glued in such a way as to present banding in two opposite directions. In fact a variety of permutations are possible, such as chevron patterns or incorporation of more than one colour of tiger's eye in one stone (figure 71). On the same basis, many other strongly marked stones can be cut and reformed and this includes many examples of attractive fossil material that will contrast well with stones of similar hardness.

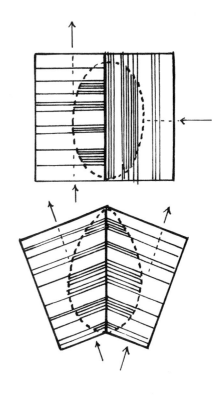

Fig 71 Patterns formed by re-assembling tiger's eye. Arrows indicate direction of fibres.

Doublets and Triplets

Precious opal is more frequently associated with composite stones of this type and allows the cutter to use flakes and fragments of stone that in other materials might be considered useless. By isolating thin seams of opal from the matrix the best use can be made of precious material, and forming doublets and triplets is often the only means of using the stone to advantage.

The brilliant fire in opal is attributed to a minutely layered structure of hydrated silica which breaks up the light spectrum into a scintillating play of colour. This can vary considerably in intensity and has a marked influence on the commercial value of the stones. As the colour is retained, and often enhanced, by skilful cutting and arrangement the formation of doublets and triplets does not greatly lessen the value of precious opal.

To minimize any loss of light filtering through the thinner seams of opal, thus detracting from the reflected spectrum qualities, it has been found that a black backing material cemented to opal flakes will retard leakage of light and return maximum colour. Since opal is a relatively soft stone ($5\frac{1}{2}$ to $6\frac{1}{2}$ Mohs' scale) a backing of similar hardness should be selected. Dark toned opal potch, black glass or the opaque varieties of dark obsidian, are frequently used and easily fashioned into the desired shape (figure 72).

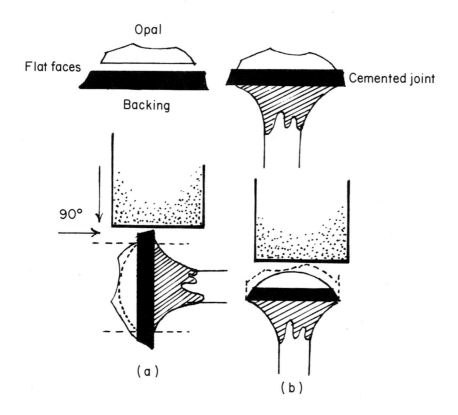

Fig 72 Preparing and shaping a doublet. (a) Establishing perimeter shape. (b) Forming the cabochon dome – girdle below cement joint.

Doublets Assorted opal pieces may contain material of sufficient thickness to form shallow cabochons, or seams of obvious fire may be associated with a matrix of sandstone or grey potch. It will be necessary to remove the matrix by grinding or slicing on a fine trim saw, using water coolant, to expose the opal layer and decide on the amount of usable material with uniform colour and fire. The slice is then sanded flat to form the upper layer of the doublet. Any matrix on the underside need not be removed entirely but must also be sanded perfectly flat to make a flush joint with the backing stone. With larger pieces of more solid opal problems of removing matrix will not arise. The stone should be examined carefully to establish the most suitable colour orientation and to decide whether the thickness will permit the cutting of a shallow cabochon. In addition the flat base section should be prepared in order to make a perfect cement bond.

There are several optional doublet shapes and the depth of the base layer can vary (figure 73). Very thin flakes of opal may need a stronger supporting layer. With a cabochon top the edges of the dome should be carried into the backing layer to bring the girdle of the doublet below the cement line. In the case of flat topped stones,

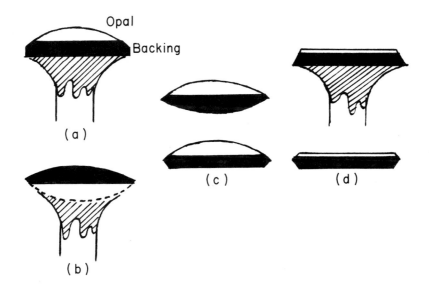

cut a bevel round the perimeter of the doublet to expose the black banding. By carrying the girdle below the bonded joint any risk of damage through pressure on claws or burnishing of a bezel during setting will be confined to the backing material.

Fig 73 Opal doublets. (a) Shaped opal cabochon. (b) Doublet reversed to shape backing layer. (c) Double and single cabochons. (d) Thin opal flakes on supporting backing layer.

When shaping a doublet it is not necessary to run the machine at full grinding speed and most of the work is possible on finer grinding wheels. It is important that the opal should never become overheated and both cutting and sanding must be done with copious water coolant, for if dehydration occurs the stone will crack and flake. Backing materials of glass and obsidian should also be ground with care, for both are brittle and have a tendency to chip or splinter. Cold dopping methods are preferable to heating and hot wax treatment.

Triplets Thin veneers of opal with exceptional qualities of colour and fire are enhanced when sandwiched between the backing layer previously described and an upper layer of transparent rock crystal shaped and polished in cabochon form (figure 74). This not only affords protection for the precious layer but also intensifies the colour hues in the opal spectrum and creates the appearance of greater depth.

The base of the rock crystal must be sanded smooth before adhesion to the flat surface of the polished opal flake. Following cementing with clear adhesive, the cabochon dome is cut and polished in the usual way. In some cases the quartz cabochon is cut and polished independently in carefully measured proportions corresponding with the opal and backing previously shaped together. On completion of the clear dome it is cemented to the opal and any refinements to the total appearance of the triplet are then finally carried out.

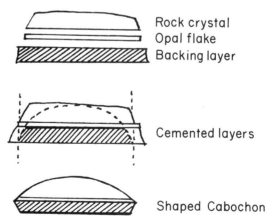

Rock crystal
Opal flake
Backing layer

Cemented layers

Shaped Cabochon

Fig 74 Forming an opal triplet.

Part Two

Facet Cutting

Gemstone cutters who are familiar with the more general lapidary techniques will find the transition to faceting quite straightforward should they wish to pursue this branch of the craft which is often regarded as the ultimate in gemcutting. There are many lapidaries for whom faceting has little or no appeal, or for some reason they believe the skills involved are beyond their capabilities. To these and also complete beginners in lapidary it must be pointed out that reasonable success with the very first stone can be assured once the mechanics have been mastered.

There are many reasons why people are attracted to faceting and perhaps the most obvious is to produce a gemstone cut in a particular style suitable for setting in jewellery. Others respond to the pure geometry of the faceted form and the technical challenge involved. For some the interest lies in cutting rare gems or those difficult-to-cut stones of both natural and synthetic origins. Among these are crystals ranging from very soft to hard, including those with multiple and complex areas of cleavage. Many of these finished gemstones form the basis of collections and are not intended for setting in jewellery.

In the chapters that follow, equipment, materials and cutting techniques are outlined, together with simple formulae for fashioning standard brilliant and step cuts. Beyond this stage additional styles derived from the basic cuts are shown in step-by-step sequences by means of cutting charts and diagrams. Angle conversions applicable to facets for different gem minerals are indicated in one of the appended tables.

5   *Specialized Equipment*

It is often said that elaborate equipment is not essential to facet gemstones and basically this is true when we consider the jamb-peg devices used by earlier cutters. Here we encounter the skill and judgment of the true craftsman who is able to assess by eye the required proportions and angles to fashion a gem style and at the same time is sensitively attuned by ear and touch to critical rates of cutting on the lap. We are not all equally gifted, however, and as we live in an age of highly developed technology there are precision instruments for faceting at the disposal of both professional and amateur cutters. Wherever possible these should be fully utilized to bring the pleasures of gem cutting within the range of all. Although many of these sophisticated machines make faceting easy, with pre-selection of facet index and angles, controlled speeds and pressures, the human element should not be discounted and the hand of the craftsman will still be evident in a well cut stone.

MACHINES

The choice of faceting machine depends on requirements and the capital outlay one is prepared to channel into the craft. Prices are generally commensurate with degrees of refinement in the equipment and it often pays to ensure that each operational phase is made simple and foolproof. Precision cutting and finishing is dependent on total stability of the unit and meticulous engineering of the finer adjustable parts. For the specialist facetor there are purpose-built machines offering a wide range of aids to successful cutting and, although functionally similar in many respects, the overall designs will vary between manufacturers (figures 75–78). Faceting head attachments supplied as accessories to general lapidary units are more simple in conception, but have the same functional merits and will enable the cutter to acquire the technical skills necessary for many of the basic cuts.

Fig 75 Ultra-Tec faceting
machine with overhead light
attached.
*Photograph courtesy Ultra-Tec
Stanley Lapidary Products,
Santa Ana, California, USA.*

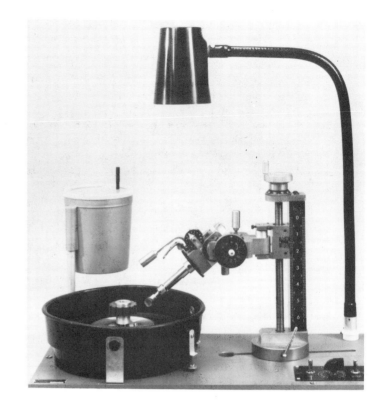

Fig 76 Faceting unit manu-
factured by Imahashi Manu-
facturing Co. Ltd, Tokyo,
Japan.
*Photograph courtesy of
Gemstones Ltd, Hull, England.*

3.   Cat's-eye and star stones

4.   A selection of faceted stones

Fig 77 Robilt Faceting Unit with assortment of dops, transfer block, cutting and polishing laps.
Rytime Robilt Pty. Ltd, Sandringham, Vic., Australia Photograph courtesy Hirsh Jacobson Merchandising Co. Ltd, London, England.

Fig 78 Glenjoy 'Concord' Faceting Unit. Variable electronic speed control. Special slide base for positioning facet head assembly.
Glenjoy Lapidary Supplies, Wakefield, England.

Cutting Laps

Laps of copper, steel, lead and cast iron have been used effectively with silicon carbide powdered grits in 400 to 600 grades on a variety of stones. Silicon carbide grits applied to cast iron laps will provide a cheap but adequate abrasive surface for cutting quartz gems and others in a lower hardness range. However, one disadvantage is that grit slurries are messy and the machine must be thoroughly cleaned at the end of each session to remove abrasive particles, particularly near bearings and working parts. Areas likely to rust must be dried and finally wiped with an oily rag.

Laps impregnated with diamond particles are more widely favoured and are standard issue with many faceting units. Copper and other soft metal alloys are manufactured with diamond grits embedded or sintered into the surface to give maximum durability and cutting life. Two laps, with coarse diamond mesh size 600 used in the preliminary stages and mesh size 1200 for refinements, are normally adequate before polishing. Water coolant or refined oils are applied to the lap as necessary during cutting. Diamond laps are faster in their cutting action, far cleaner in use and free of the risk of grit contamination that is present when silicon carbide grits are used.

Lap surfaces can also be charged by the lapidary with diamond compounds in similar mesh sizes to those mentioned above and these are supplied in syringe applicators and used with special extender fluids or light oils. Diamond compounds are frequently colour coded by manufacturers and are supplied in a range of micron sizes.

Micron Size	Grit Mesh Size
1	14000
3	8000
6	3000
15	1200
30	600
45	325

Polishing Laps

Polishing discs are cut from various hard materials such as thick acrylic sheet, copper, tin-faced and type-metal laps. Scoring of the surface is helpful in some cases to retain the polishing oxides but is not always advantageous. Sharp burrs on scored metal laps must be levelled off before use to prevent the danger of badly scratched facets (figure 79). Other laps can be made of hardwood sealed with beeswax, or muslin and closely woven canvas stretched over firm supports and impregnated with wax to give a smooth surface. Polishing laps should be firm, to avoid too much resilience in the surface where pressure on the stone may result in rounding over of facet edges. Phenolic laps are generally recommended for soft stones.

Polishes are applied to the laps as water-based slurries and tin oxide, cerium oxide, chrome oxide are used in varying circumstances. Compounds such as Linde A are beneficial on certain stones either as a pre-polish or final polishing medium. Cerium oxide on an acrylic lap is an excellent general purpose polish and ideal for quartz gems and many others. (See table of lap surfaces and polishes, page 135).

Fine micron diamond compound, 8000 to 14000 mesh size, forms an alternative polishing medium and is particularly suited to harder gemstones, for example corundum gems respond to diamond polishes used on a finely textured vinyl lap.

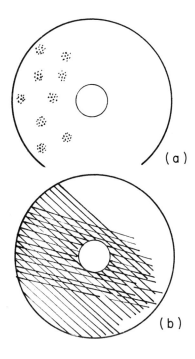

(a)

(b)

Fig 79 Preparing lap surfaces. (a) Cutting and sanding lap. To impregnate with diamond compound apply sparingly in series of dots from applicator and spread with finger. Apply pressure from hard roller or agate slab to embed diamond particles. (b) Polishing laps scored with sharp knife. Raised burrs must be removed before use.

6 Gem Minerals

Faceted stones are usually cut from minerals of defined composition and structure, conforming to specific crystal systems. Selection is based on optical properties such as clarity, colour, brilliance and dispersion, present in varying degrees, and stones are cut scientifically to enhance some or all of these qualities. For this reason it is important to clarify some of the factors which may influence choice of gem rough and the appearance of a finished stone.

Cleavage Degrees of toughness and hardness in crystal forms result from tight or loose bonding of the structural atoms. Where loose bonding exists the weakness produces a possible cleavage plane, or in some cases cleavage in more than one direction. Stones cut from crystals with pronounced cleavage in known directions must be orientated so that the table of the gem is a few degrees out of parallel with the plane of weakness, Topaz is a good example of perfect basal cleavage while fluorite will cleave in four directions.

Fracture, as distinct from cleavage, is a more random form of breakage which occurs in characteristic manner depending on the mineral composition. Examples of these are the shell-like conchoidal fracture seen in quartz and obsidian, and hackly or splintery fractures found in tough fibrous minerals.

Refraction The speed of light passing from the air to solids, as in the case of a gem crystal, is considerably reduced and the direction of the light path is changed to different degrees in certain minerals. Differences are scientifically measured to provide a refractive index (R.I.) and gem styles are designed to suit the R.I. of a particular mineral, for example the standard brilliant cut is suited to clear stones with highly refractive properties. The resultant brilliancy is the amount of light transmitted back to the eye, being reflected internally from the pavilion facets when these are cut at the correct angles (figure 80).

Dependent upon the crystal structure, some gems are doubly refractive, that is the light ray splits in two on entering the stone and each ray has a different index of refraction. On close examination through the table of such a cut stone, a doubling of the back facets will be seen. Differences between the refractive indices in a particular gem is known as birefringence.

Dispersion White light entering a crystal is split into component spectrum colours, each travelling at a different wavelength speed and index of refraction. The bending of the coloured rays to varying degrees is called dispersion. Good dispersion in a gemstone is the ability of the particular mineral to separate the spectrum wavelengths in order that they can be returned to the eye with maximum colour or 'fire'.

Specific Gravity Although having little influence on the actual cutting of a stone, the density or specific gravity (S.G.) can determine the size of a gem in ratio to carat weight. However, specific gravity is of greater importance to the gemmologist as a means of identification. A simple test to determine the density of a gem is to immerse the stone in heavy liquids with known specific gravities. Stones with a S.G. lower than the liquid will float near the surface or sink if the S.G. is higher. When the density of the stone and liquid are evenly matched the stone will be suspended at a fixed level.

SELECTION OF ROUGH GEM MATERIAL

Clarity in a gem crystal is of paramount importance, whether colourless or tinted, and the absence of flaws and inclusions greatly enhances the appearance and value of a cut stone. Many minerals of natural origin formulate minute flaws and inclusions during normal structural growth and attempts to isolate clear workable areas often result in a stone of small proportions. Imperfections can sometimes be concealed by a setting if they are placed off-centre under the pavilion girdle facets. In a similar way patchy colouration can be minimized by placing the coloured zone in the lower portion of the pavilion where possible. This may even provide an added depth of colour to the stone.

Crystals should be examined carefully against a strong light, turning the rough slowly in the fingers. Internal

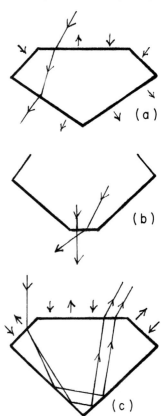

Fig 80 Path of light rays in cut gems. (a) and (b) Loss of light in badly cut stones through shallow pavilion angles and wide culet facet. (c) Light transmitted back to eye in correctly cut gem.

fractures and inclusions can often de detected in this way by the interruption of light rays passing through the stone. It is helpful to wet the rough or apply a thin fim of colourless oil when viewing. Difficulties arise when broken outer surfaces of the crystal prevent a clear passage of light and reflect a confusing irregularity of outline within the crystal. To overcome this, immerse the stone in a liquid of similar refractive index which will make the crystal edges barely visible. By shining a concentrated beam of light through the container any cracks or imperfections in the crystal will be revealed by deflection of the light rays. A list of immersion fluids for this purpose is given in the appendices.

Brilliant cut styles are more often suitable for colourless or lightly tinted crystals, relying on refraction and dispersion of white light as already described. Coloured stones are enhanced by step and mixed cuts in varying depths – for example deeply coloured stones will benefit from shallower proportions and weaker hues may sometimes be intensified by greater pavilion depths and increasing the number of stepped facets.

Many gem crystals have a high degree of colour absorbency and owe their specific hues to the selection of particular coloured wavelengths in white light. This results in isolation of the gem colour, with the rest of the spectrum being absorbed within the crystal. Individual colours transmitted in this way may vary the tint and intensity when viewed under different light sources. Absorbency characteristics in some crystals show two colours when viewed from different directions and are termed 'dichroic', or 'pleochroic' when more than two colours are visible. Stones cut from these minerals will require selective orientation to display the desired colouration. Good examples of minerals showing this property are iolite and tourmaline.

SOME GEM MINERALS TO FACET

H = hardness on Mohs' scale   R.I. = refractive index

Andalusite H.$7\frac{1}{2}$
R.I. 1.63–1.64

Green, greenish-brown

Apatite H.5
R.I. 1.64

Green, yellow, blue, colourless

Beryl Varieties H. $7\frac{1}{2}$–8

Emerald R.I. 1.56–1.59 — Deep green

Aquamarine R.I. 1.57–1.58 — Blue to green

Morganite R.I. 1.58–1.60 — Rose to salmon pink

Chrysoberyl H.$8\frac{1}{2}$
R.I. 1.75–1.76

Alexandrite – red/ green
Shows colour change, green in daylight, red in artificial light

Corundum H.9
R.I. 1.76–1.77

Ruby – deep red
Sapphire – pale to deep blue

Dioptase H.5
R.I. 1.64–1.71

Deep green

Epidote H.$6\frac{1}{2}$
R.I. 1.73–1.77

Yellow, green, brown
Perfect basal cleavage

Fluorite H.4
R.I. 1.43

Colourless, yellow, green, blue, purple
Perfect cleavage in four directions

Garnet Varieties

Grossular (Hessonite)
H.$7\frac{1}{4}$ R.I. 1.74 — Red, brownish-orange

Pyrope
H.$7\frac{1}{4}$ R.I. 1.73–1.75 — Red

Almandine
H. $7\frac{1}{2}$ R.I. 1.78–1.81 — Red, brown

Spessartite
H.$7\frac{1}{4}$ R.I. 1.79–1.81 — Red, orange

Andradite (Demantoid)
H.$6\frac{1}{2}$ R.I. 1.88 — Green

Kyanite H.5–7
R.I. 1.71–1.73

Blue. Hardness change with directional orientation.
Perfect cleavage

79

Peridot H.6½
R.I. 1.65–1.68

Yellow, green, brown

Quartz varieties H.7
R.I. 1.54–1.55

Rock crystal – colourless
Amethyst – purple
Citrine – yellow
Smoky – brown

Spinel H.8
R.I. 1.71–1.73

Pink, red, pale to deep blue, purple

Spodumene H.7
R.I. 1.66–1.67

Kunzite – lilac,
Hiddenite – green, yellow, perfect cleavage

Topaz H.8
R.I. 1.63–1.64

Colourless, blue, pink, pale green, yellow, brown.
Perfect basal cleavage

Tourmaline H.7–7½
R.I. 1.62–1.64

Deep green, red, blue, pink, black

Zircon
High type H.7–7½
R.I. 1.92–1.98

Low type H.6½
R.I. 1.78

Colourless, blue, green, yellow, brown.
High dispersion

SYNTHETIC GEMSTONES

Corundum H.9
R.I. 1.76–1.77

Synthetic ruby and sapphire. Also in colours simulating
danburite, rose topaz, tourmaline, alexandrite etc.

Rutile H.6–6½
R.I. 2.62–2.90

Colourless. High dispersion

Spinel H.8
R.I. 1.72

Wide range of colours simulating aquamarine, peridot,
tourmaline, red spinel and zircon.

Strontium Titanate H.6
R.I. 2.41

Colourless. No natural counterpart. High dispersion

Yttrium Aluminium Garnet
H.8–8½ R.I. 1.83

Colourless, red, green. No natural counterpart.

Fig 81 Synthetic boules of
corundum and spinel.

7 Working Sequences

Fig 82a Assortment of metal dop shapes: 1. Flat top for table areas, 2. Hollow, conical dop for tapering pavilions, 3. V section or wedge-shaped dop for step cut pavilions, 4. Flat face plate used as an aid to alignment during transfer.

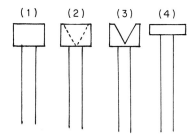

Fig 82b Conical dop for tapered pavilion. (a) Dopped stone must have all round clearance. (b) Stone should be resting on metal dop secured by displaced wax. (c) Stone should not be elevated on excessive wax.

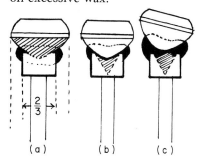

Pre-forming Gem crystals rarely come in large sizes but the use of a trim saw, preferably with a thin blade, may be needed to isolate material for more than one stone or establish a rough shape. Additional shaping can be done on a silicon carbide grinding wheel, where the hardness of the stone will allow, to pre-form the required gem style (figures 96 and 105). Where the stone is too small to hold in the fingers it can be dopped on a wooden stick as for cabochon cutting. Grinding must be done with extreme care to prevent formation of any fractures in the crystal and copious water coolant should be used. Pre-forming may also be done on a horizontal lap with loose grits using a water-based slurry with a little detergent added. If a diamond lap is used in pre-forming there is danger of damage to the lap surface through gouging with sharply pointed areas of crystal.

Dopping Decide whether to start by cutting the crown or pavilion facets, which is often a matter of personal preference. In some instances it is helpful to cut pavilion facets first and dop the pre-form accordingly. This enables inspection through the table or upper facets when cutting the crown following transfer to the second dop, particularly in stones where the pavilion culet is not central.

Select the appropriate metal dop to suit the shape of the gem (figures 82a and 82b). Heat both dop and stone and fill the dop with molten wax. Push the stone into the dop to displace surplus wax in the case of conical or V dops and mould a firm support under the pavilion pre-form. Make sure that none of the wax will interfere with cutting of the girdle.

Shaping the Girdle Insert the dop into the faceting arm and set the angle at 90 degrees and parallel to the lap. Lower the head on the stand rod until the stone meets the lap surface. Release the locking device to allow the arm to rotate freely in the case of round girdles and cut until perfectly circular and symmetrical. With rectangular step cuts, adjustment of heights will be necessary when squaring up the ends and sides of the stone. During cutting the stone is moved across the lap in a horizontal side-to-side motion for a short distance to prevent wear on the lap in one place. This applies throughout all stages of cutting and polishing (figure 83).

Fig 83 Rounding the girdle pre-form. Index trigger released to allow free rotation of facet arm.

The Table. This is usually the largest facet of any gem and often the most difficult to polish. Set the faceting arm at 45 degrees and insert the 45 degree angle adaptor. Place the dop in position as shown in figure 84(a)(b). Lower the faceting head until the stone touches the lap and cutting is felt as it is moved from side to side, then lock in position. This positioning is done with the lap stationary. Cut the table to the required width for this stage using the coarse lap, followed by refinements on

Fig 84a Cutting the gem table. Dop secured in 45 degree angle adaptor.

Fig 84b Detail of 45 degree angle adaptor.

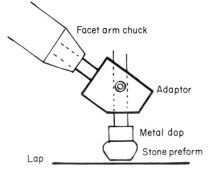

Facet arm chuck

Adaptor

Metal dop

Stone preform

Lap

83

the finer lap, and also continue through and carry out the polishing phase. If the polish lacks uniformity this can often be remedied by removing the dop from the machine and polishing on a felt or leather lap with cerium oxide on a standard cabochon unit, holding the metal dop in the fingers. This invariably brings up a highly polished table surface.

Main and subsequent facets. Main angles for crown and pavilion portions of the gem are calculated to allow maximum values of light refraction, governed by the refractive index of the gem crystal. Slight deviation in angles is permissible but in the pavilion these must not fall below the accepted critical angle – this will result in loss of light through the back facets, diminishing the internal reflection and giving a lifeless gem which lacks sparkle or fire. The internal play of light is further assisted by symmetrical arrangement of other facets making up the gem style and the whole is calculated to retain this scintillating play within the geometric unit. In addition the highly polished outer planes contribute their own reflective lustre when the stone is moved in different positions against the source of light.

Techniques During the side-to-side cutting action there are variable speeds involved. The outer, peripheral edge of the lap is moving at a faster speed than areas towards the centre of the disc. A check must be made on the different cutting rates of the facets, which in turn are affected by hard and soft parts or directional grain in the crystal structure. Results of this may show in the timing or rate of cutting for different facets in the same row. This can lead to overcutting of certain facets if constant inspections are not carried out with a 10x magnification loupe to ascertain progress.

Providing the facets are correctly positioned and the angles finally established to complete a series, it may not be necessary to link up adjacent facets when using the coarse cutting disc. Sharp edges and points can be achieved on the finer disc with less danger of over-cutting.

Records When working from established cutting charts, double check the index settings and required facet angles on the machine before starting to cut. Where, for any reason, deviations or adjustments have to be made these must be recorded for reference and repetition during later stages.

Adjustments However meticulous the cutter may be with his settings it does happen, through different cutting speeds, structural factors in the stone or varying pressure on the faceting arm, that a facet fails to spread evenly in one direction or some parts remain unpolished. This can be rectified by either the use of the index tooth splitter (cheater) or fine height adjustment, which minutely changes the areas of contact between facets and lap surface in forward, backward or lateral movements. The corrective actions are illustrated in figure 85.

Fig 85 Left : Fine height adjustment. *Right :* Use of index splitter (cheater).

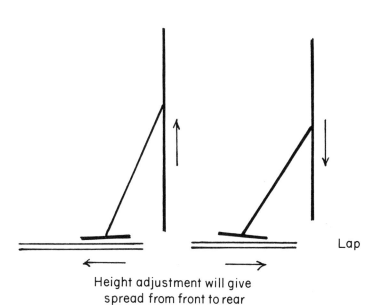

Height adjustment will give
spread from front to rear

Polishing Following two cutting stages, which is the norm in most cases, the stone should be polished with whatever polishing medium is preferred. The facets are generally polished in reverse index sequence to that used in cutting. If cerium oxide is used on scored laps the consistency must be sufficiently fluid to allow free movement of the gem. Laps overloaded with thickened slurries will cause the mixture to adhere to facet surfaces on the stone, causing it to slide across the lap rather than polish. Also, as the polishing oxide dries out through frictional heat, it forms hardened granules under the stone which are capable of scratching the partially polished facets. Paper tissues should be kept at hand to wipe the stone at each inspection with the loupe. Only proceed to the next facet or series of facets when a flawless finish has been achieved.

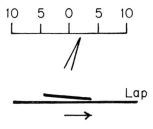

Action of cheater spreading surface
contact of facet either left or right

85

Transferring the Stone To reverse the stone for cutting the opposite set of facets it has to be transferred from the old dop to a new dop in order to expose the uncut portion of the pre-form. This is done with the aid of a transfer block constructed with two 'V' grooves for accurate alignment of the dops. During transfer, care must be taken to line up main facets on crown and pavilion where this is necessary. Most metal dops are designed with a securing feature such as a notch or small projection which engages in the chuck of the faceting arm. The transfer block supplied with the machine will repeat this locking feature and allow the dops to be aligned correctly.

Clamp the dop into position in one half of the 'V' block, heat a new dop filled with melted wax and clamp loosely into the opposite 'V' groove. Re-heat the wax of the new dop and also warm the stone, then slide the new dop until the wax is pressed firmly against the gem. The new dop may require re-heating to soften the wax displaced by the stone so that it can be firmly moulded in position. Remove both dops, still linked securely by the wax and with the gem in the middle, and heat the old dop until the wax softens and can be pulled away from the stone without dislodging its new position. (*See photographic sequences,* figures 86–89). Surplus wax adhering to the stone must be cleaned off by gently scraping with a heated knife point and wiping with methylated spirit.

Dislodged Stones Very occasionally a stone may become dislodged from the dop during cutting and, alarming as this may be, it is possible to re-dop the stone in its previous position. One of the principal causes of losing the stone from the dop is by accidentally catching it on the edge of the lap, or allowing the facet arm to drop too quickly onto the lap surface. Too much pressure and heat generation during polishing may cause softening of the dop wax and will also contribute to loss of stones from the dop. In many instances the occurrence of dislodged stones follows transfer dopping when one half of the stone has been highly polished and adhesion to the wax is lessened. For this reason some cutters prefer to use a cold dopping method with two-part epoxy dough instead of wax on the new dop.

As soon as the stone becomes detached remove the dop carefully from the chuck without disturbing any of the wax on either dop or stone. The imprint of the facets or general shape of the stone will still be clear in the hardened wax, conversely the wax sticking to the stone

Fig 86 Transfer sequence. Old dop with stone, *right*, and new dop, *left*, being heated gently in spirit flame.

Fig 87 Slide together and press crown table into melted wax of new dop. Allow to cool.

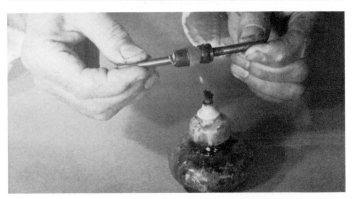

Fig 88 Remove dops from transfer block. Heat wax and metal shank of old dop to release stone.

Fig 89 Stone released and transferred to new dop in readiness for cutting pavilion facets.

will match the portion where it has broken away. Place the stone back in position on the dop and it will be found that the two parts correspond exactly as before. Hold firmly and place marks of alignment on the stone and metal part of the dop to make sure of the position. Heat the dop in a spirit lamp flame for a brief period to partially melt the wax without losing the shape of the matching cavities. Heat the wax on the stone for a second then quickly bring together in the correct position and a bond will be formed. Return the bonded stone and dop to the flame once again, continuing to press in position until the wax has reformed and the stone is once more secure. If necessary add further droplets of hot wax and mould round the stone to reinforce the original wax. Allow to cool thoroughly before starting to cut.

Continued Cutting Sequences Follow the ordered sequence of the cutting chart, commencing with the main facets as before and then complete the rest of the facets for the particular stone. Polish all the facets in reverse order. Finally, polish the girdle which in some cases will also be faceted according to the gem style.

The Finished Gem Detaching the stone from the dop and cleaning to remove traces of wax is always an eagerly awaited moment. At this point the inherent gem qualities of the mineral will be fully revealed and a critical assessment of personal skill and judgment can be made.

To remove the stone, heat the metal dop near the waxed end until the wax softens sufficiently to release the stone. Warm the tip of a pointed knife or similar instrument and gently push away remains of the wax still sticking to the stone. This is much safer than scraping at the stone or chipping away hardened wax. Cleaning can be done with methylated spirit which is a reliable solvent for shellac based dopping wax. A wash in warm water and detergent will degrease the stone which should then be dried and rubbed on a soft cloth to bring up the gem sparkle. Avoid too much handling to prevent transfer of greasy prints; the gem can be picked up with tweezers for inspection.

8 *Standard Round Brilliant*

During cutting it is important to use appropriate machine speeds and cutting laps and apply lubricant as necessary. The stone must not be placed in contact with the lap until the motor is switched on, except for checking and height adjustment purposes. The direction of the lap rotation is clockwise with a trailing cutting action and not head on to the stone.

Cutting sequences for crown and pavilion facets are shown in the diagrams (figures 90 and 91) and the angles given are for quartz, using a 64 tooth gear. A conversion chart showing numerical sequences and relative index positions for 96, 64, and 48 index gears is given in figure 92. Main facet angles for minerals other than quartz are appended in Table 5.

Cutting the Crown Carry out the preparatory stages outlined previously, such as pre-forming, dopping and shaping the girdle. Cut and polish the table to about 70 or 65 percent of the total width of the pre-form. The main facets will further reduce the size of the table to 50–45 percent, which can be adjusted by increasing or decreasing the main angle slightly if circumstances warrant it.

Main Facets Refer now to the cutting chart and note the sequence of facets and corresponding index positions, eight in number. Set the correct angle and engage the index notch 0/64. Cut the first facet for a short period, then index the opposite facet at 32 and cut for a similar length of time. Next cut facets three and four, indexed at 16 and 48, and continue cutting opposite facets in this way with repeated checks for alignment and symmetry. Carry out finer adjustments, using decreasing pressures for a fraction of a second, to link the eight facets evenly in sharp ridges from table to girdle. The pattern of the table area should now be a regular octagon with equal sides. Remember to record any corrective changes for subsequent stages. Two abrasive stages should be used to cut the main facets but do not polish until the remainder of the crown facets are completed.

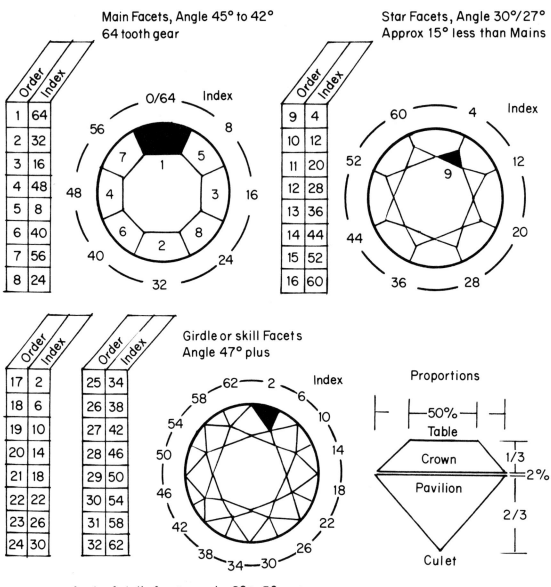

Main Facets, Angle 45° to 42°
64 tooth gear

Order	Index
1	64
2	32
3	16
4	48
5	8
6	40
7	56
8	24

Star Facets, Angle 30°/27°
Approx 15° less than Mains

Order	Index
9	4
10	12
11	20
12	28
13	36
14	44
15	52
16	60

Order	Index
17	2
18	6
19	10
20	14
21	18
22	22
23	26
24	30

Order	Index
25	34
26	38
27	42
28	46
29	50
30	54
31	58
32	62

Girdle or skill Facets
Angle 47° plus

Proportions

50%
Table
Crown   1/3
Pavilion   2%
           2/3
Culet

Angle of girdle facets can be 2° to 5°
more than mains angle,
or even higher in large stones

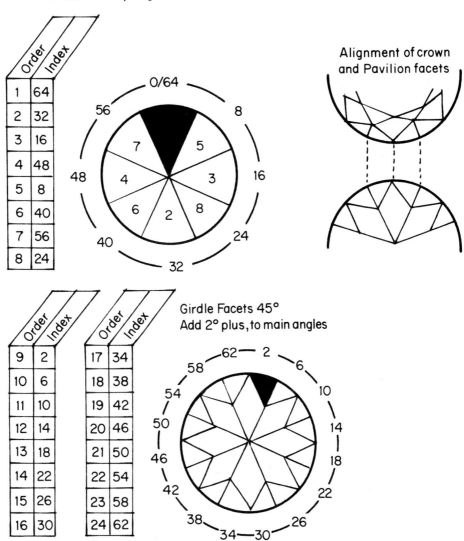

Main Facets, Angle 43°

Order	Index
1	64
2	32
3	16
4	48
5	8
6	40
7	56
8	24

Alignment of crown
and Pavilion facets

Order	Index
9	2
10	6
11	10
12	14
13	18
14	22
15	26
16	30

Order	Index
17	34
18	38
19	42
20	46
21	50
22	54
23	58
24	62

Girdle Facets 45°
Add 2° plus, to main angles

Fig 92 Conversion chart showing relative index positions for 96, 64, 48 index gears.

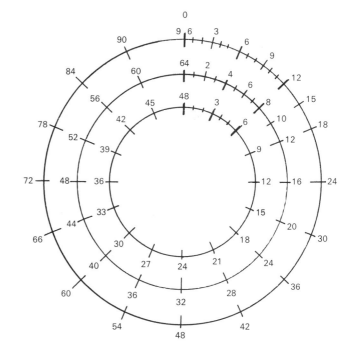

Fig 93 Dop in position for cutting crown facets.

Fig 94 Facet head accessory designed to fit an all purpose unit.

Star Facets These are minute inverted triangles which cut across the corners made by the main facets touching round the table. The triangular points reach about one third down the main ridge lines. It may only be necessary to use one abrasive stage (finer grade) to cut these small facets.

Index positions are halfway between the settings for the main facets – for example commence at index 4 followed by 12 and so on as indicated on the chart. Obtain the required angles at approximately 15 degrees less than those used for the mains.

Lower the faceting arm until the stone is able to touch the lap while it is still stationary and make a light sweep across the surface. Raise the stone and check the point of contact for orientation which, if correct, will indicate the starting point for the series. Lift the faceting arm clear of the lap before switching on the motor. Start the first cut with a single light sweep on the revolving lap for a fraction of a second, lift and inspect. The star facets are so small that a single touch may be sufficient to complete the cut. If over-cutting occurs correction may only be possible by re-cutting the main facets and reducing the proportion of the stone.

Angles may need to be adjusted to ensure that the spread of the facets will meet at the table in the centre of the mains, and that the inverted points will reach along the ridges to the required depth simultaneously. To check cutting progress and establish the correct pattern cut two adjacent facets for a short time, alternating between the two to arrive at the angle most suited to requirements. This angle must be carefully recorded. The rest of the star facets can then be cut in rotation around the table.

Break Facets (also referred to as skill facets) These are sixteen in number and are cut as triangles placed at each side of the mains ridges with the base forming the girdle and the apex approximately two thirds of the crown height and touching the points of the star facets. Starting angles can be set at 47 degrees but the final requirements, once established, may be a few degrees more or even less depending on the angles of the main and star facets.

Begin with the first pair of facets at index positions 2 and 6. Cut with a light touch for half a second, lift and wipe the stone clean with a soft tissue, then closely inspect the initial cuts with the aid of a magnifying lens. Study the shape of the triangles and estimate the rate of

Fig 95 Adjustments needed to obtain correct angle reading.
(a) Facet shape indicates that the lower spread will reach centre of girdle before touching point of star. (b) Upward spread of facet will touch star too rapidly.
(c) Facet shape spreading in correct proportion to touch point of star and centre of mains simultaneously.

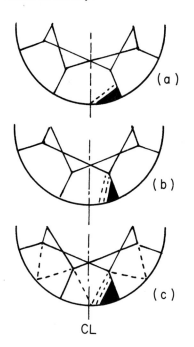

spread. If the apex is cutting too rapidly and meets the star facet before the base joint reaches the centre of the main facet the angle will need adjusting (figure 95). Increase the angle by a few degrees and index two different facets. Repeat the action until the correct angle is found and the facet points coincide at the stars and at the girdle. Complete the rest of the facets in rotation, also correcting the trial cuts. Record the angle accurately, which can be retained at that setting for finer cutting if needed and for polishing.

Clean up the stone to carry out a final inspection of the entire crown facets which should now be evenly proportioned, sharply cut and have a smooth satin sheen ready for polishing.

Polishing the Crown Facets Apply polish to the rotating lap. Lower the stone and polish each of the break facets in turn, inspecting frequently in a good light. Use moderate to light pressures and avoid over-polishing since there is a danger of dragging the surface of the gem and rounding off the sharpness of the facet ridges. As previously mentioned, this can often be the result of allowing oxide slurries to dry out on the lap, building up a concentration of dry powder on the leading facet edges.

When the break facets are completed, re-set the angle required for the star facets and polish as before. Follow by polishing the main facets at the recorded angles. Bear in mind that the index tooth splitter or cheater may have to be brought into use during these final stages. Clean the stone and make ready for transfer dopping to cut the pavilion.

Pavilion Main Facets Calculate the angle for the eight pavilion mains a few degrees less than those used for the crown mains, starting at 43 degrees for quartz. Variations will show in stones of different proportions and the final angle for a particular gem will be found through trial and subsequent adjustments to arrive at the ideal pavilion depth.

A similar index sequence to the crown mains can be used, starting with 0/64 followed by 32, alternating between opposite pairs until the facets terminate at a central point and forming sharply cut ridges along the length. Cut each facet a little at a time to control the overall symmetry, avoiding the temptation to cut one facet the whole distance in a single operation – this could lead to an off-centred pavilion, also to different thicknesses at the girdle. The broad ends of the triangular faces should stop evenly around the stone to leave a girdle thickness of about 2 per cent of the stone's width. Avoid a razor-sharp girdle which is likely to chip and crumble when gripped in a claw setting. Make allowance for a second cutting stage that will further reduce the girdle thickness.

Pavilion Girdle Facets These are positioned at each side of the main ridges and form as elongated triangles with the wide spreading edges linking at the girdle and the points touching on the main ridges about half to two-thirds between girdle and culet.

Set the cutting angles two to three degrees higher than the main angles, starting at approximately 45 degrees, and allow for progressive adjustments increasing the angle as required. Record the correct angle required to complete the series, enabling touching facets to spread gradually at the girdle to meet the centre of each main facet and progress along the ridges to the desired distance. Carry out constant appraisal of the rate of cutting and aim at a symmetrical and clean cut gem. One cutting grade may be sufficient to achieve desired results and prepare the way for polishing. Clean up the stone and exposed parts of the dop. Remove the cutting lap and replace with the polishing lap.

Polishing the Pavilion Do not alter the previous cutting angle. Polish the girdle facets in rotation, observing usual precautions and polishing techniques already outlined. Re-set the angle as recorded for the main facets and polish the remainder of the pavilion.

To polish the girdle, position the faceting arm parallel to the lap with angle pointer at 90 degrees and lower the stone onto the revolving lap surface. Release the locking device to permit rotation in the case of a round stone or index at the correct positions for a faceted girdle. Remove stone from the dop and clean thoroughly.

9 Brilliant Cut Styles

The following three cuts, illustrated by working charts and diagrams, are among several of their kind based on the crown pattern of a standard round brilliant with certain modifications. Although arrangement of the crown facets is similar in most cases, the relative shapes and proportions of the facets and table areas are affected by differences in the girdle outline of the stones (figure 96). Pavilion facets are also subject to changes and alternative forms within the requirements of critical angles for the selected gem minerals.

Having successfully cut more than one standard brilliant and acquired sufficient expertise to work out the angles and correctly position the sixteen skill or break facets, cutting these additional modified styles will not be difficult. In the light of this, detailed instructions are minimized and the experienced cutter will be able to follow the sequences and information shown in the working charts for each style. Quartz angles will be used throughout for the sake of uniformity and indexing will be based on the 64 index gear. Reference should be made to the appended tables to determine the angles required in cutting alternative gem minerals and the comparative index positions for different gear systems if required.

Fig 96 Brilliant cut styles. *Top :* Girdle outline shapes. *Centre :* Pre-forms. *Bottom :* Profile shapes.

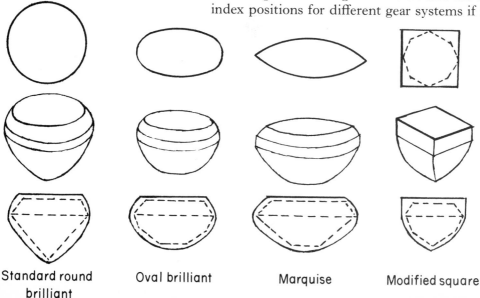

Standard round brilliant   Oval brilliant   Marquise   Modified square

THE OVAL BRILLIANT

Whereas the standard round brilliant is favoured for white or lightly tinted stones, the oval styles are particularly suited to coloured gems. Also larger stones can be cut from the rough, utilizing portions of the material that would otherwise be trimmed away in a circular pre-form. The girdle proportions of the oval will determine the facet index positions which are subject to slight changes with different ratios of width to length. With practice and careful judgment the index requirements and also suitable angles can be modified during cutting. Index positions given in the cutting charts, (figures 97 and 98), and working descriptions will be found suitable for oval stones with a ratio of one to two or just slightly wider. As the width increases index changes will become necessary to suit particular needs.

Pre-forms and Dopping

Select the table area for the stone and grind a flat surface to the extent of the desired girdle. This will make scribing an oval perimeter much easier. Mark on the length and width of major and minor axes to a two to one ratio, bearing in mind that these are the widest limits of the oval. The rest of the perimeter should be linked in even curves. If drawing an eliptical shape free-hand onto the stone is found to be difficult, it may help to cut out a template from stiff card and draw round the shape. The overall depth of the rough should allow for a pre-form of one-third to the crown and two-thirds pavilion, as in the case of a standard brilliant.

Carefully grind to the oval perimeter shape, allowing the edge to form an even girdle at right angles to the flat table area and thick enough for the height of the crown. Draw a line round the stone at approximate crown depth, keeping it parallel to the flat rim, and grind a bevel down to the line. This is to provisionally establish a straight edge for the girdle to act as a guide when cutting the main and skill facets. Avoid making the bevel too pronounced or anticipating the crown main angles.

Various methods are used to form a straight girdle edge and shape the oval. Some cutters prefer to do this with the dopped stone in the facet head of the machine, cutting a series of skill or break facets to an even depth around the stone. The angles for these facets are merely tentative and will be modified at a later stage. Shaping is also done by indexing the positions of the break facets with the facet arm set at 90 degrees and cutting a series of girdle edge facets to form an approximate oval shape of

OVAL BRILLIANT   Crown facets
Consecutive cutting order

Fig 97

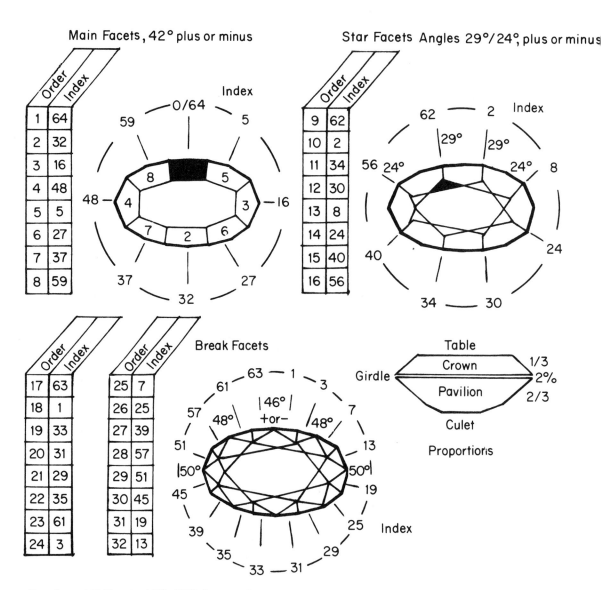

Main Facets, 42° plus or minus

Order	Index
1	64
2	32
3	16
4	48
5	5
6	27
7	37
8	59

Star Facets Angles 29°/24°, plus or minus

Order	Index
9	62
10	2
11	34
12	30
13	8
14	24
15	40
16	56

Order	Index
17	63
18	1
19	33
20	31
21	29
22	35
23	61
24	3

Order	Index
25	7
26	25
27	39
28	57
29	51
30	45
31	19
32	13

Break Facets

Table
Crown   1/3
Girdle   2%
Pavilion   2/3
Culet

Proportions

Break or skill Facets 46°- 50° plus or minus.
Girdle edge facets indexed in same positions.

98

OVAL BRILLIANT Pavilion Facets
consecutive cutting order

Fig 98

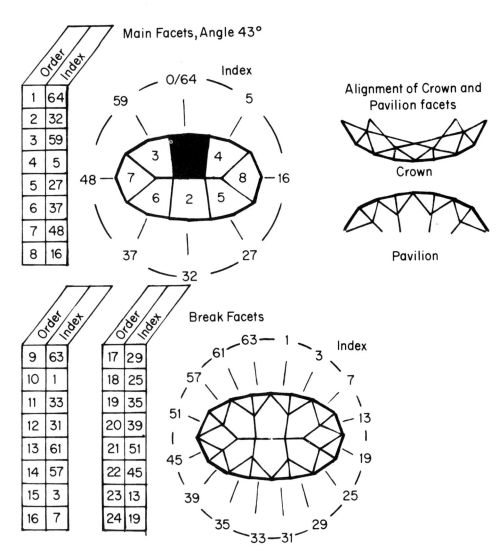

Main Facets, Angle 43°

Order	Index
1	64
2	32
3	59
4	5
5	27
6	37
7	48
8	16

Alignment of Crown and Pavilion facets

Crown

Pavilion

Order	Index
9	63
10	1
11	33
12	31
13	61
14	57
15	3
16	7

Order	Index
17	29
18	25
19	35
20	39
21	51
22	45
23	13
24	19

Break Facets

Break or skill Facets, 45° plus

even proportions. Once again this need not be a finalized girdle perimeter.

To complete the hand pre-forming, roughly shape the pavilion, tapering from the long sides and the ends as shown in figure 96 to a proportionate two-thirds depth, allowing a generous girdle thickness at this stage. Secure the pavilion portion of the pre-form in a 'V'-shaped dop to cut the crown facets, with the long side of the pavilion resting along the 'V' groove. The diameter of the dop should permit free access to the girdle area, also making allowance for displaced wax to be moulded under the stone. The table area should be horizontal and at right angles to the dop shank.

Insert the dop into the faceting arm but, before tightening the chuck, lower the arm, with the angle at 90 degrees and indexed at 0/64, until the long side of the dopped stone rests on the cutting lap. Allow the dop to turn freely in the holder until the stone touches in a central position, then tighten the chuck. Switch on the machine and take brief cuts at indexes 64, 32 on the long sides and 16, 48 at the ends of the stone. Check to see if the major and minor axes are centred and line up across the stone, and also to see if the ratio still checks out. Unlock the chuck to carry out any adjustments that may be necessary, and re-tighten ready for cutting.

The index diagrams illustrated are arranged with the long axis of the stone lying parallel to the lap when indexed at 64, 32. It is possible with some machines that the V dops with a special locking notch or peg for engaging into the chuck will only position the ends and not the sides of the stone on the lap at the indices mentioned. In such cases, secure the dop just short of the locking notch to place the stone in the correct position, failing that, relative index positions will have to be substituted for those shown.

The Table

Set the faceting arm at 45 degrees and insert the dopped stone into the 45 degree angle adaptor. Lower the arm until the stone rests on the lap but lift clear before switching on the machine. Cut the table level and carry out two cutting stages until the surface is smooth and free from scratches. Attach the polishing lap and polish the table to a mirror finish.

Main Facets

Cut the eight main facets at the index positions shown on the working chart with the angle set at 42 degrees for quartz. Cut down evenly towards the pre-formed girdle line, or until the table area has been reduced to 75 per cent and is centrally placed. Check the total symmetry of the table shape and the corresponding facet junctions. Replace the coarse cutting lap with the finer one and re-cut the eight main facets to a pre-polish stage. The fine lap can remain in position for the rest of the crown facets as it is usually adequate for cutting the tiny star and break facets.

Star Facets

Cut the first pair of star facets indexed at 62, 2, with the angle set at 29 degrees, a reduction of 13 degrees from the main angles. The small triangular facets cutting across the corners of the mains ridges will meet in the centre of the main facet at the table and the inverted points reach about one third down the ridge lines. Cut a little at a time to assess the direction of the facet spread to meet requirements and be prepared to make slight angle adjustments. Index the opposite pair of facets at 34 and 30 and cut the second pair of star facets at the same angle. The four remaining facets will fall on the sharper curves of the oval towards the ends of the stone and have slightly less spread at the table to meet the other longer side facets. The angles will have to be reduced to about 18 degrees less than the mains, for example to 24 degrees. Index as indicated in the cutting order, 8, 24, 40, 56. Obtain the new angle and correct height adjustment for each facet, cutting a little at a time to check progress until satisfied that the angle is adequate to complete the series of star facets.

Break or Skill Facets

Index the sixteen facets as shown on the cutting chart, and although an order of cutting has been suggested this is not necessarily an unalterable sequence. As a starting point on the long sides of the oval, cut adjacent pairs indexed 63, 1 and opposites 33, 31. Set a temporary angle of 50 degrees for the first pair and cut a little of each facet for a brief second. Examine through a magnifying lens and check the spread of the facets which, if correct, should cut into the main facet and meet at a central point on the girdle and simultaneously touch the tips of the star facets. This will probably be accomplished at 50 degrees but could be fractionally plus or minus according to variations in the basic oval shape and proportions of the crown. To give a fixed angle for these break facets would be misleading, as for their counterparts in all brilliant cut styles. The angles must be accomplished gradually and personal judgment alone will hit on the correct ones to complete the perfect cuts. With oval brilliants the angles required towards the ends of the stone may differ a few degrees to those on the longer sides.

A height adjustment will be necessary for each change of angle and index position around the stone, which should be tested on the stationary lap before continuing cutting. Always remember to keep a careful record of final angles and any relevant changes for later modifications if needed and for final polishing.

Girdle Edge Facets

As indicated earlier, a faceted girdle may already have been cut provisionally during pre-forming stages when shaping the oval girdle. These facets may now be slightly out of alignment with the completed break facets and will require adjustment.

To facet the girdle, position the faceting arm at 90 degrees and lower the stone in contact with the lap. A change of height will be needed for each indexed position which repeats those previously used for the break facets. The ridges of each adjoining face around the girdle should coincide accurately with the points of the break facets.

Polishing

Retain the 90 degree angle and polish the girdle. Follow the usual order for polishing the crown facets at the pre-recorded angles. The completed crown can now be thoroughly cleaned and made ready for transfer dopping.

THE OVAL PAVILION

Alternative pavilions are possible for the oval brilliant; these include the standard pointed culet and the wedge-shaped styles. Of the two the wedge mains variety, of which there are several modifications, is more suited to the optical qualities of coloured stones as the main facets are all cut to acceptable angles for total internal reflection.

As the pavilion facets are relatively simple to execute, detailed cutting instructions are not necessary and reference to the working charts will show at a glance the positions of the facets and overall design. Following transfer, set the dop in the correct position so that the main facets can be cut to coincide with those of the crown at the same index numbers.

Main Facets

Set the angle at 43 degrees for quartz and cut two opposite facets indexed at 64 and 32 until the required girdle thickness is reached. The facets should meet in a sharp wedge to form a horizontal line parallel to the girdle and in the centre of the stone on the long axis. Centring can be controlled more effectively by cutting a little of each facet alternately.

Cut the four facets at each side of the two central mains, indexed at 59, 5, 27, 37, ensuring even proportions. Spread the facets to line up at the girdle and centre ridge. The sharp ridge at the junction of the opposite pairs will no longer be parallel to the girdle.

Follow by cutting the remaining two main facets indexed at 16 and 48 to continue the girdle line at the broad end. These should taper to touch the previous facets in a sharp point and in continuous alignment along the central axis. Repeat all the above facets on the finer cutting disc.

Break Facets

These are cut to align with those on the crown and match up with the girdle edge facets. Adjacent facets will meet at points about half way along the mains ridge line and touch at the girdle in the centre of the mains. There are sixteen break facets as in the crown and similarly indexed. Retain the fine cutting disc and set the angle a few degrees higher than the mains, at about 45 degrees for trial cuts. Try out the first pair of facets indexed at 63, and 1 and examine the triangular spread. If the angle needs to be increased by a few degrees index the opposite pair of 33, 31. When the correct angles have been established complete the opposite pairs 63, 1, and 33, 31. Then index to left and right 61, 57, 3, 7 and 29, 25, 35, 39, to establish a linking pattern (*see index diagram*).

The remaining four facets at the ends of the stone, indexed 51, 45, and 13, 19, will probably require a change of angle increased by a few degrees. Check this carefully by cutting a little at a time until the facets meet at the respective points.

Polishing

Retain the last angle reading and polish the two end facets. Re-set at the previous angle and polish the series of break facets. Complete the pavilion by polishing the main facets at the correct angles. Remove the stone from the dop and clean thoroughly.

THE MARQUISE CUT

Sometimes referred to as the Navette Cut, this is a more elongated stone than the oval cut, with pointed ends formed by the intersection of two curves which gives the distinctive girdle outline to this stone (figures 99 and 100). A ratio of two to one, the length between the points being twice that of the width, will give a suitably proportioned stone and with the crown and pavilion depths similar to those previously used for brilliant styles.

Pre-forming

Establish a flat table area and shape the girdle approximately to the desired outline. Allow sufficient depth for crown and pavilion portions of the stone, with a generous girdle thickness, and roughly indicate the crown and pavilion outlines (figure 96). The correct shape will be established during cutting and excess rough will be removed on the coarse lap to give the required main angles.

Dop the pre-form on the pavilion side, using a V dop with a smaller diameter than the girdle of the stone to prevent interference during cutting. The elongated shape will project beyond the dop at both sides and should be given additional support underneath by building up the dopping wax towards the points to counteract leverage which might unseat the stone.

The Crown Table Facet

With the faceting arm set at 45 degrees insert the dop into the 45 degree angle adaptor and cut the table, using two lap stages, coarse and fine, to about 75 per cent of the stone's width. Remove the cutting lap and polish in the usual way.

Main Facets

Referring to the cutting charts it will be seen that the facet positions around the curvature of the stone require changes of angles in order to attain a uniform depth down to the girdle. These angles can be reduced by the cutter if desired to alter facet proportions and overall appearance of the stone, and also diminish the size of the table accordingly. Changes in the main angles will, of course, influence the angles of all the supporting facets. It is for this reason that quite often different angles for the same cuts are quoted in books on faceting, but to dispel any confusion it is pointed out that these are usually the outcome of personal preference in the gem styling on the part of the cutter. However, it should be remembered that too much deviation from the accepted main angles for a particular mineral will lead to disappointing results. The charts and instructions given here will enable the cutter to produce a presentable stone on the two to one proportion and will form the basis for any later changes in shape and size.

The order of cutting shown is not mandatory but it is helpful to cut opposite pairs on a rotational basis for balanced shape control. The two main facets, indexed at 0/64 and 32 to place the long sides of the stone in contact with the lap, are cut at 42 degrees for quartz and the rest of the facets at a few degrees plus or minus according to position. Thus facets 3, 4, 5 and 6 on the chart, indexed at 5, 27, 37, 59, are cut at approximately 36/44 degrees. The two end mains 7 and 8, indexed at 48 and 16, are cut at about 27/30 degrees, adjusting the height for each change of index. Pre-shape on the coarse grit disc followed by refinements on the finer lap.

Star Facets

As these are quite small the finer lap should be left in position for cutting. The eight stars are numbered on the chart in order of cutting, with 1 to 4 indexed at 62, 2, 30, 34, and cut at the same angle of approximately 22/26 degrees. The correct angle will enable the facet pairs to meet in the centre of the mains to form a reduced table edge. End facets, pairs 5, 6, and 7, 8, indexed at 56, 40, 8, 24 are all cut at about 16/22 degrees and will meet the centre stars at the table half way along the mains. Any angle changes must be recorded. The table width will now be reduced to about 50 per cent.

Break Facets

It should be possible to retain the fine cutting lap for these facets. The sixteen facets, indexed as shown on the chart, are cut in series of four sharing the same angle settings. The angles given are once again only approximate and an adjustment of a few degrees either plus or minus may be needed to position the facets accurately round the stone. As always with the break facets, brief trial settings may be necessary on two or three different facets in order to judge the required direction of spread at the edges and points of the facets in order to meet accurately. Having once found the correct angles they must be recorded.

Faceted Girdle

Set the arm at 90 degrees and place the stone in the re-

MARQUISE CUT   Crown Facets   *Fig 99*
Consecutive cutting order
Index positions for
ratio of 2–1 proportions

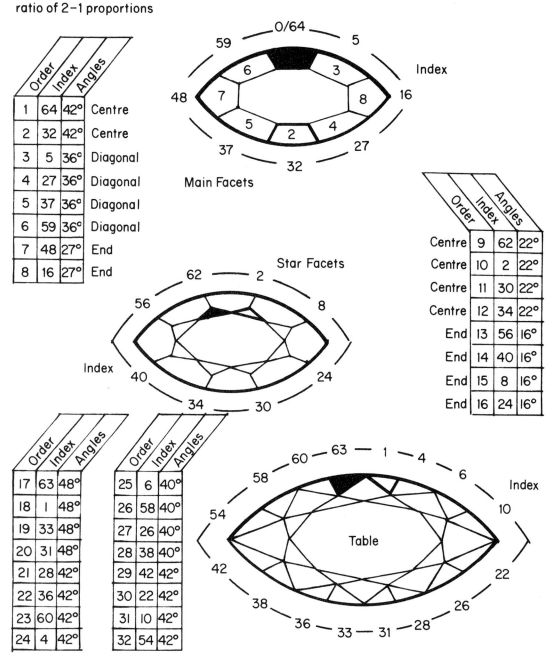

Order	Index	Angles	
1	64	42°	Centre
2	32	42°	Centre
3	5	36°	Diagonal
4	27	36°	Diagonal
5	37	36°	Diagonal
6	59	36°	Diagonal
7	48	27°	End
8	16	27°	End

Main Facets

Star Facets

Index

	Order	Index	Angles
Centre	9	62	22°
Centre	10	2	22°
Centre	11	30	22°
Centre	12	34	22°
End	13	56	16°
End	14	40	16°
End	15	8	16°
End	16	24	16°

Order	Index	Angles
17	63	48°
18	1	48°
19	33	48°
20	31	48°
21	28	42°
22	36	42°
23	60	42°
24	4	42°

Order	Index	Angles
25	6	40°
26	58	40°
27	26	40°
28	38	40°
29	42	42°
30	22	42°
31	10	42°
32	54	42°

Table

Index

Break or skill Facets. Angles given are only approximate starting points.
Final angles may be plus or minus a few degrees.

Fig 100

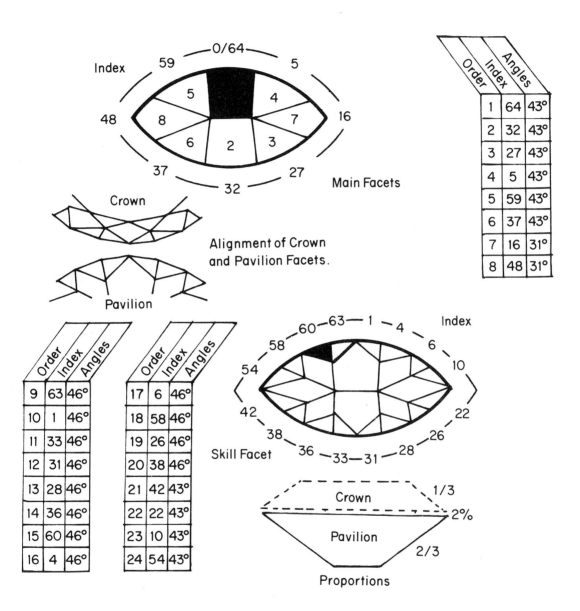

Main Facets

Order	Index	Angles
1	64	43°
2	32	43°
3	27	43°
4	5	43°
5	59	43°
6	37	43°
7	16	31°
8	48	31°

Alignment of Crown
and Pavilion Facets.

Crown

Pavilion

Order	Index	Angles
9	63	46°
10	1	46°
11	33	46°
12	31	46°
13	28	46°
14	36	46°
15	60	46°
16	4	46°

Order	Index	Angles
17	6	46°
18	58	46°
19	26	46°
20	38	46°
21	42	43°
22	22	43°
23	10	43°
24	54	43°

Skill Facet

Crown

Pavilion

Proportions

1/3

2%

2/3

Break or skill Facets. Adjust angles if needed,
plus or minus a few degrees.

quired position on the lap. Cut the girdle facets indexed as for the break facets, adjusting heights as necessary round the curvature of the stone. The girdle facets should align accurately with the break facets.

Polishing

Keep the faceting arm angle at 90 degrees, attach the polishing lap and complete the girdle facets. Follow by polishing the facet series either in the original order of cutting or in reverse order as preferred. Inspect each facet carefully through a magnifying lens to ensure a flawless polish.

Pavilion Facets

Transfer the stone onto a flat dop of the same diameter as before, leaving the girdle clear and free from wax. Insert the dop into the faceting arm and at index 64 position the long side of the stone parallel to the lap. Prior to locking the dop firmly in position, precise alignment is made by indexing one of the girdle facets, 1 or 63, and placing flat on the lap surface.

Main Facets

Raise the facet arm and set the angle at 43 degrees for quartz and cut the six main side facets as indicated on the chart, indexed at 64, 32, 27, 5, 59, 37, adjusting the heights for each facet. Facets 1 and 2 in the cutting order should meet at a sharp ridge in the centre of the stone and at the same time establish a suitable girdle thickness at the previously polished edge. If the girdle edge is reached before the ridge is formed, or vice-versa, adjust the angle slightly to rectify the fault. Cut the other four main facets to produce a continuous edge at the girdle and parallel thickness.

Raise the height of the stone to cut the two end mains, indexed at 16 and 48, and change the cutting angle to about 31 degrees. Complete the main facets on both coarse and fine laps, establishing a sharply defined pattern as shown in the diagram.

Break Facets

The index positions will be the same as those for the crown break facets and the girdle facets to assure precise alignment. Approximate angles are given as a starter in the cutting chart but these may require a plus or minus adjustment. Cut in a similar order as indicated until adjacent facets meet and exact alignment with the girdle facets is achieved. The points of the facets should reach down about half way along the mains ridges.

Carry out the final polishing phase to complete the pavilion, remove the stone from the dop and clean thoroughly.

MODIFIED SQUARE BRILLIANT

Pre-form the rough with a square girdle and allow sufficient material for crown and pavilion proportions of one-third to two-thirds overall depth (figure 96). Taper the pavilion slightly to facilitate dopping but main angles should not be anticipated at the pre-form stage. Until this particular cut has been made more than once and the cutter is able to assess the shape of the finished stone it is better not to pre-shape the crown area, other than levelling off the surface to remove any rough parts of the crystal. Also the eight-sided girdle shape should be cut on the faceting machine, indexed at the correct positions, since any attempt to judge these positions in the rough pre-form may result in wastage of material and ultimate reduction in the size of the gem.

Dop the stone on the pavilion end in a conical dop that is two-thirds the width of the stone to leave the girdle clear. Insert the dop in the 45 degree adaptor and cut and polish the table in the usual way.

Forming the Girdle

Set the faceting arm at 90 degrees and square up the stone accurately at 0/64, 32, 16, 48 indices. Cut the eight sides as illustrated, indexed at 2, 14, 18, 30, 34, 46, 50, 62, until they are of equal length and the perimeter shape is perfectly symmetrical. This can be controlled by cutting opposite pairs a little at a time until the junction ridges are aligned centrally on opposite sides of the stone. Repeat on the fine lap. Polishing of the girdle can be done now or at a later stage as preferred. Refer to cutting charts (figures 101, 102).

Crown Main Facets

Cut four main facets at 45 degrees, indexing opposite pairs 64, 32, and 16, 48. Reduce the table width to about 70 per cent of the stone's width ensuring that all four sides of the resultant square are equal in length. The sequence is repeated on the fine cutting lap. Retention of the fine diamond lap may be sufficient to complete the rest of the crown facets on small stones.

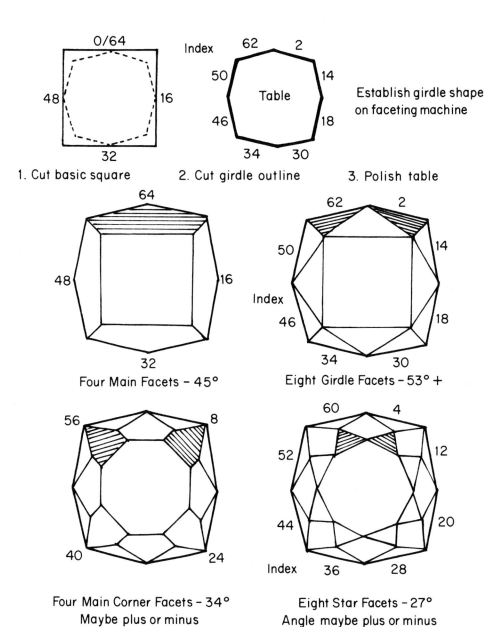

0/64

48   16

32

1. Cut basic square

Index   62   2

50   14

Table

46   18

34   30

2. Cut girdle outline

Establish girdle shape
on faceting machine

3. Polish table

64

48   16

32

Four Main Facets – 45°

62   2

50   14

Index

46   18

34   30

Eight Girdle Facets – 53° +

56   8

40   24

Four Main Corner Facets – 34°
Maybe plus or minus
a few degrees

60   4

52   12

44   20

Index   36   28

Eight Star Facets – 27°
Angle maybe plus or minus
a few degrees

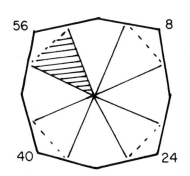

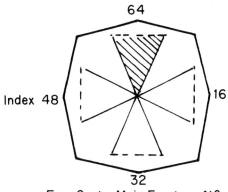

Index 48

Four Main Corner Facets – 41°

Four Centre Main Facets – 41°

Eight Girdle Facets – 55° – 58°

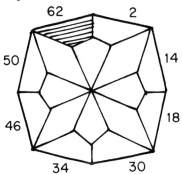

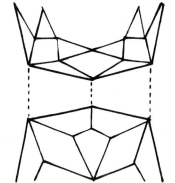

Alignment of Crown and Pavilion
girdle facets

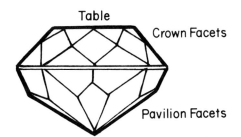

Table

Crown Facets

Pavilion Facets

Girdle Facets

These are eight in number; they can be cut in pairs and indexed in rotation, for example 62, 2; 14, 18; 30, 34; 46, 50. Cutting angles may vary in individual stones from approximately 53 to 58 degrees.

Index 62 and start cutting the first facet at 53 degrees for a brief second, lift and inspect. The facet should show a spread towards the centre point at the girdle and reaching the corner point of the square table. Where this is in doubt do not proceed any further but cut the next facet in the pair, index 2, increasing the angle by one or two degrees. Cut briefly and inspect as before. Continue this procedure until the correct angle is found then cut the rest of the facet pairs in rotation. Adjacent facets at this stage will meet in a V point on the centre of the main facet at the girdle and will touch at the corners of the table. The main facets will be reduced to triangular shapes flanked by pairs of girdle facets (*see diagram for progressive patterns of the crown facets*).

Main Corner Facets

There are four of these indexed at 8, 24, 40, 56, and as before, depending on the dimension of the stone, the required angles will vary. Set 34 degrees as a starting point but the final angle may be plus or minus a few degrees. Remember to keep a record for the polishing stages.

Aim at cutting the corner facets at the widest part, the same dimension as the other four main facets, to create an octagonal table. The points of the facets should reach the girdle but care must be taken not to over-cut beyond the girdle line.

Star Facets

Eight crown star facets (*see diagram for relative positions*) are indexed at 4, 12, 20, 28, 36, 44, 52, 60.

Tentatively cut at 25 degrees to 27 degrees around the star positions, or adjust further as required either up or down a few degrees. The completed facets should touch at the table in the centre of the main facets and be of equal length to retain a regular octagonal table. The opposite points will form a sharp junction with the upper edges of the girdle and corner facets. The corner facets will become kite-shaped as the stars cut across the upper edges.

Retain the same angle and polish the star facets, followed by the rest of the series in reverse cutting order. Clean up the stone and carry out transfer dopping to cut

Fig 103 The faceted styles featured. *Left :* Brilliant cut range. *Top to bottom –* Standard Round, Oval, Marquise, Modified Square. *Right :* Step cut range. *Top to bottom –* Emerald Cut, Cardinal Cut (stepped pavilion), Keystone Cut, Kite Cut.

the pavilion. Be sure to select a new dop that will allow a good elevation of the stone's girdle.

The Pavilion
It is important that the eight girdle edges will lay true on the lap face at the indexed positions for the girdle facets. Test each in turn at 90 degrees on the stationary lap, rotating the faceting arm. Adjust the dop in the holder if necessary.

Corner Main Facets
Cut the four corner facets at 41 degrees, indexed at 8, 24, 40, 56. Carry the facets down to the girdle line taking care not to over-cut the desired girdle depth. The facets may or may not terminate in a sharp culet point at this stage.

Centre Main Facets
These are cut at the same angle of 41 degrees at index positions 64, 32, 16, 48, and should be cut to form a sharp culet point in this case, completing also the terminations of the previous corner main facets in the process. It is not necessary for the centre main facets to reach the girdle as they will be cut to the correct shape by the girdle facets.

Girdle Facets
Index in pairs at 62, 2; 14, 18; 30, 34; 46, 50; where there should be an exact corresponding match with the crown girdle facets. Trial cuts will have to be made to establish the correct angles which should be in the region of 55 to 57 degrees.

Concentrate on the corner points of the facets at the girdle where they cut into the corner mains to form a sharp V. Spread along the girdle line so that adjacent facets of each pair will meet as a ridge half way across the centre main facets, at the same time spreading towards the pavilion point. (*Refer to diagrams of pavilion facets.*)

Following fine cutting, complete the polishing sequences in reverse order. Before removal from the dop the girdle edge should be polished at 90 degrees, where this was not done previously, taking care not to lose any of the sharpness of the crown and pavilion facets bordering the girdle.

10 *The Step Cut*

THE EMERALD CUT

Perhaps the best known version of the step cut is the Emerald Cut with its series of parallel facets on both crown and pavilion and a rectangular girdle shape. Designed for coloured stones of every hue and intensity, this cut enhances the larger stones by means of deep pavilions and increased rows of facets which produce a scintillating pattern of light through the stone. The large crown facets permit maximum entry of light to give full value to the refractive properties of the gem mineral and also reflect external bands of light from the polished faces.

Basic Features

The crown can have two or three angled facets stepping up from girdle to table. Pavilion facets can be three to six in number or even more if the depth of the stone allows. The culet can terminate in either a sharp ridge or a narrow facet. Proportions are usually determined by the cutter according to size, number of facets and allowance for orientation, but the main facets are constant for the particular mineral.

Characteristic dimensions for the emerald cut are: crown one third of the total height, pavilion two thirds of the height, split into horizontal bands. The first of these, next to the girdle, may be cut to half the depth of the pavilion and the second cut to half the depth of the girdle facet. Second and third facets are often of equal depth. Any further facets are planned to suit the remaining depth of the pavilion (figure 104).

Pre-forming

By careful pre-forming minimum wastage of gem material is incurred. As a prelude, any sharp points and hollows should be ground away to allow better assessment of the total mass for orientation. Avoid over-shaping at the pre-form stage or any attempt to antici-

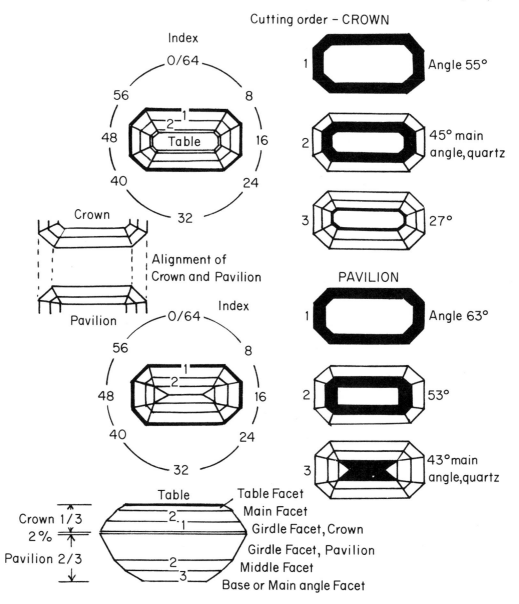

Cutting order – CROWN

Index

0/64

56   8

48   Table   16

40   24

32

1   Angle 55°

2   45° main angle, quartz

3   27°

Crown

Alignment of Crown and Pavilion

Pavilion

PAVILION

1   Angle 63°

Index

0/64

56   8

48   16

40   24

32

2   53°

3   43° main angle, quartz

Crown 1/3
2%
Pavilion 2/3

Table

Table Facet
Main Facet
Girdle Facet, Crown
Girdle Facet, Pavilion
Middle Facet
Base or Main angle Facet

Crown facets 1 and 2, approximately same height
Table facet, half or less than mains.

Pavilion facets – Girdle, approximate height of Crown or
       half height of pavilion.
       Facets 2 and 3, half height of girdle facet

pate facet angles and allow a generous outward curve on all four sides of both crown and pavilion areas once the desired proportions have been established (figure 105). The dopped pre-form should be free from excess wax with the girdle clearly exposed for cutting.

Fig 105 Step cut styles. *Top* – girdle outline shapes, *Centre* – pre-forms. *Bottom* – profile shapes.

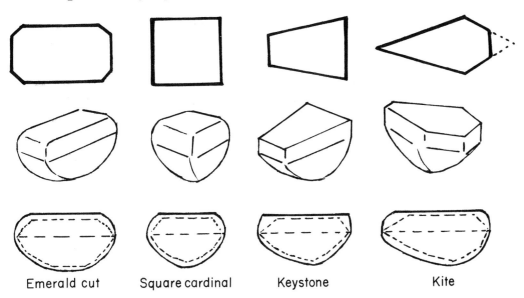

Emerald cut	Square cardinal	Keystone	Kite

Shaping the Girdle

Secure the dopped stone in the chuck of the faceting arm and set the angle at 90 degrees, indexed at 0/64. Lower the stone with the long side in contact with the lap and cut a perfectly flat face. Index at 32 to place the opposite long side on the lap and cut for a similar period until flat and parallel to the first side. To cut the two ends, raise the faceting head a little until the stone rests on the lap at index position 16, followed by 48, and cut opposite ends until parallel and the flat planes meet those at the sides. Continue until the corners meet at right angles, which need not be sharply defined where corner facets are to be added. Cut the corners in rotation, indexed at 8, 24, 40, 56, matching the length of each cut and linking in parallel bands with the four sides (*refer to cutting chart,* figure 104).

Cutting the Pavilion

The principal angles mentioned for pavilion and crown facets are those most suitable for quartz. Angle variations for other gem minerals are shown in Table 5. Use one or two cutting stages as needed but it will be found that small stones and facets can be cut on the finer lap in one operation.

Cutting parallel facets requires some expertise as the facet junctions must correspond sharply along adjacent sides of the stone in continuous lines (*see* figure 106). If a facet edge is developing out of parallel, or the polish is not uniformly distributed over the entire facet, corrections can be made by using the index tooth splitter and height adjustments (figure 85). Where these actions occur the angles may change very slightly and details must be recorded to ensure correct repetition.

Fig 106 Position of stone on lap to cut parallel facets. (a) Minimum side to side movement. (b) Facet arm traversing too widely. Facet will cut at different rates.

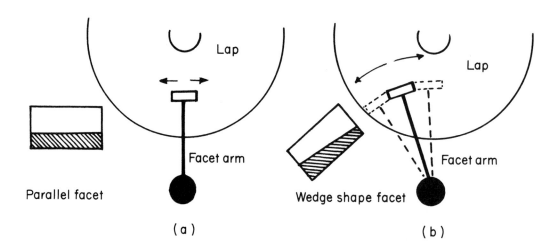

Parallel facet — Lap — Facet arm

(a)

Wedge shape facet — Lap — Facet arm

(b)

To cut facets bordering on the girdle set the angle at 63 degrees, index 0/64, and adjust the height to place one of the long sides in contact with the lap. Raise the stone before switching on the machine, then lower the stone and commence cutting. Spread the facet gradually to approximately half the pre-form depth and pay attention to the edge approaching the girdle to avoid over-cutting material needed for the two per cent girdle thickness and proportionate amount for the crown. Index the opposite long side at 32 and cut the second girdle facet. Follow by cutting the ends and corner facets, ensuring horizontal link-up of the eight facets around the stone.

The order of cutting is not standardized in any way and some cutters prefer to cut long sides first and then corners and ends in strict rotation, aligning the facets accordingly. Difficulties arise when cutting the last girdle facet to achieve precise continuity and manipulation techniques of index splitter and micro-height adjustment may have to be used.

The second row of facets, once again eight in number, including corner facets, can be cut at 53 degrees and indexed as before. Spread the facet depths to about half that of the girdle facets and maintain constant checks on parallel edges. It will be seen that corner facets are tapering towards the base at this stage and, depending on the stone's proportion and number of facets, will probably terminate in small triangles at either the second or third row.

The third and final row of facets in a pavilion limited to three rows will be main facets and cut at 43 degrees for quartz. If the corner facets have been worked out the main facets will number only four, two long and two short, forming a sharp corner ridge. Index for the two sides and ends as before. Ensure that the facets are running parallel and the culet ridge is forming in a central position. At this last stage it is advisable to cut opposite sides a little at a time with frequent checks to control the symmetry. Clean up the stone and machine and replace the cutting lap with the polishing lap.

Polishing the Pavilion

Retain the last cutting angle and polish the main facets. Working in reverse order towards the girdle, polish the other rows at appropriate angles and index positions, allowing for any adjustments recorded. Repetition of any split indices and height variations will have to be made to spread the polished surfaces evenly. This may also be achieved by increasing the pressure on the faceting arm or using different positions on the lap. Complete the series by polishing the girdle at 90 degrees. When a flawless polish has been added to each facet the stone should be cleaned and the dop removed from the chuck in readiness for transfer. Measure the total depth on the pavilion from culet to girdle to work out the proportionate height of the crown.

When setting the stone in a new dop test the level on a horizontal surface while the wax is still soft and manipulate the stone so that the long edge will lay perfectly flat on the lap. Set in such a way that the index sequences for the long sides and ends are the same as before to avoid any confusion. A similar alignment check can be used on all stones with straight-sided girdles.

Cutting the Crown

The height of the crown from girdle to table can now be calculated (it will be approximately one third of the total depth of the stone), and the position of the table established. Set the arm at 45 degrees and secure stone and dop in the 45 degree angle adaptor. Lower the stone onto the lap and cut the table down to the required level. Use two stages of cutting for this larger facet surface which must be flawless, follow immediately by polishing to a high finish. Once this is done it will be possible to see into the stone and observe the position of the back facets. This is useful as a double check on parallel alignment for subsequent crown facets.

Remove the 45 degree adaptor and reset the angle to cut the broad facet next to the girdle at 55 degrees, indexing opposite sides at 64 and 32. Cut the ends and corners, linking up the adjoining ridges to give even thickness round the entire girdle which is now reduced to 2 per cent of the stone's depth.

Reset the angle at 45 degrees and cut the eight main facets in the same order as before. At this stage the main facets may also have joined up to the table. A third and final set of facets cut at a lower angle will reduce the size of the table and depth of the main facet. The angle for this facet will vary from 27 degrees or less, according to the desired area of the table. In many cases the third facet is merely a narrow strip bordering the table and can be omitted in very small stones. When the table facet is cut to a depth of one third of the main facets, the overall reducing proportions of the crown facets will have a pleasing relationship.

Polishing the Crown

The three sets of crown facets are polished in reverse order, starting at the narrow table facet, then the mains and finally the girdle facets. Carry out a final inspection, remove the stone from the dop and clean carefully.

THE SQUARE CARDINAL CUT

This style is sometimes called the Double French Cut (figure 107). As shown in the diagram, the pavilion is step cut and the crown designed as a four-rayed star with split or double facets along the points. The main facets are placed along four sides of a square making twelve crown facets in all, not including the table. The pavilion is in three steps on each of the four sides, also numbering twelve facets. As the crown facets are relatively large,

SQUARE CARDINAL CUT. Stepped Pavilion

Fig 107

Cutting order 1. Square girdle at 90° index 64,32,16,48.
2. Cut and polish table. Follow with crown and Pavilion sequences

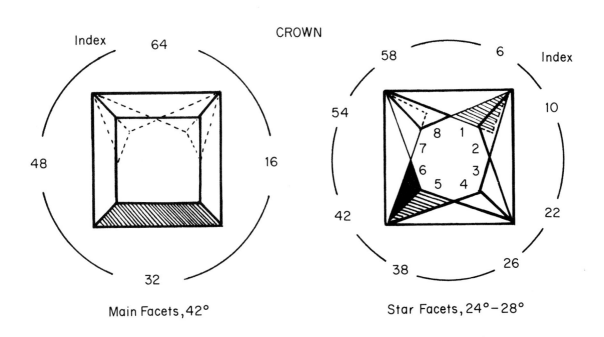

CROWN

Main Facets, 42°

Star Facets, 24°–28°

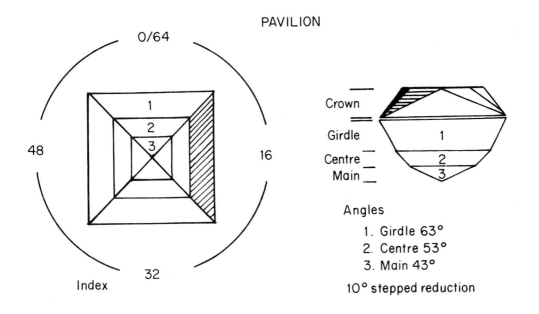

PAVILION

Angles

1. Girdle 63°
2. Centre 53°
3. Main 43°

10° stepped reduction

allowing considerable entry of light into the stone, this particular cut is suited to deeply coloured stones.

Pre-forming

Cut a square girdle, allowing for completed proportions of one third and two-thirds depth above and below the girdle. Do not taper the pavilion pre-form sharply but leave an outward curve to the four sides (figure 105). Dop the stone with a good clearance to the girdle areas and free from wax. Square up the four sides accurately on the faceting machine, set at 90 degrees, and carry out both coarse and fine cutting stages.

Cutting the Crown

Move the angle to 45 degrees, insert the adaptor and dopped stone to cut and polish the table. The table should be a little over two-thirds of the total width of the stone at this stage. With the polishing lap still in position, return to 90 degrees and polish the four girdle edges.

Main Facets

Select the appropriate angle for main facets, for example 42 to 45 degrees for quartz, the lower number usually being more suitable for crown mains in coloured quartz stones. Index as shown in the cutting chart and cut opposite pairs, 64, 32, 16, 48, alternating to retain the square table with sides parallel to girdle edges. Use two cutting stages to prepare the surface for polishing.

Corner or Star Facets

These are eight in number, cut in pairs to form a centre ridge and tapering to points at the girdle at each of the four corners. The broad ends of the facets link to form a hexagonal table.

Referring to the diagram, index the four pairs in the following order, 6, 10, 22, 26, 38, 42, 54, 58. Find the appropriate angle, which can vary between 20 degrees and 28 degrees depending on the previous dimensions. Start at a higher degree rather than lower to make a test cut and observe the developing shape of the facet through a lens. If the angle is too high the point of the facet will reach the girdle corner too soon. Gradually reduce the angle to spread the facet at the table area to a point where it meets an adjacent facet in the centre of the main and simultaneously touches the girdle corner (figure 108). It will be seen that the first facet of each pair cuts across the corner of the square table and spreads well beyond the mains ridge. This is corrected by the

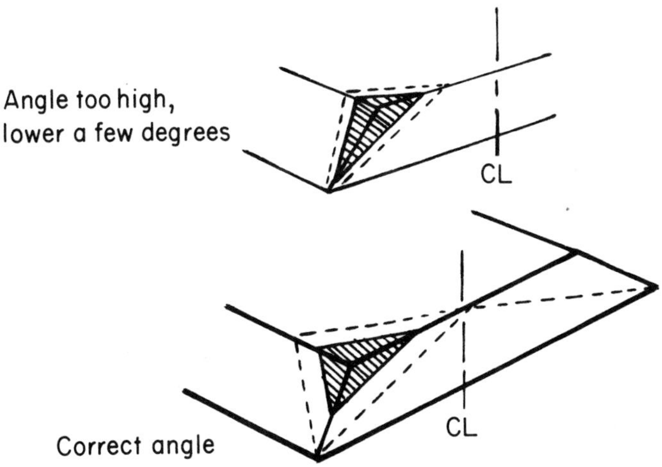

Angle too high,
lower a few degrees

CL

Correct angle

CL

Fig 108 Angle adjustment to
obtain corner facet.

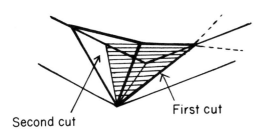

Second cut

First cut

Fig 109 Corner or star pairs.

second facet which over-cuts the first to create equal
proportions and centralizes the tapering point (figure
109). The main facets will eventually become triangular
in shape.

Once the correct angle has been found do not proceed
to completion with any of the pairs before the others have
been started and are at the same stage. Allow a little
margin for correction and possible readjustment of the
angle to make the sides of equal length to form a regular
hexagon. It may only be necessary to use the finer
cutting disc to form these smaller facets, dispensing with
the coarse stage.

Polishing the Crown
Retain the angle and polish the eight corner facets. Re-
set the angle to complete the four main facets. Carry out
dopping transfer in readiness to cut the pavilion.

Pavilion Facets

Insert the new dop into the chuck and set the angle at 90 degrees. Lower the arm until it touches the lap and ensure that the girdle of the stone sits squarely on the lap. Failure to check this may result in the long pavilion facets being out of parallel to the girdle edge. Adjust as necessary before finally securing the dop.

Step 1: Set the angle at 63 degrees to cut the broad facets next to the girdle. Index in rotation 64, 16, 32, 48, aligning the facets round the stone and reducing the girdle thickness gradually to two per cent of the stone's total depth. Do not over-cut. Cut the facet to a depth of half the total distance between girdle and culet.

Step 2: Cut the next row of facets to half the depth of the previous facets at an angle of 53 degrees. Ensure parallel alignment and sharp junctions at the corners. Avoid wide sweeps across the cutting lap to prevent formation of curved or wedge-shaped facets (figure 106).

Step 3: The remaining four facets, cut at quartz main angle of 43 degrees, will terminate at the culet point.

Finally, complete the polishing stages in reverse order, working from the point towards the girdle.

11 *Step Cuts with Off-set Pavilions*

The following two cuts, kite and keystone shapes, have the pavilion points off-centre on the long axis. This places the deepest part of the stone, viewed from the side, under the broad part of the table axis in the case of the Kite Cut, and well up into the wider portion in the Keystone Cut (figures 110 and 111). Both pavilion and crown are step cut in a series of parallel facets which echo the girdle outline of these particular styles.

Stones of this type are rarely cut for ring settings and because of their geometric outlines form decorative units in themselves. Often they are used as single drop pendants, ear-drops, or are incorporated into more elaborate necklace settings. Coloured materials lend themselves to step cuts of this kind and stones of smaller dimensions can be worked from irregular pieces of gem rough that might otherwise be unsuitable for more symmetrical types of cut.

Pre-forming

Pre-form as shown in the diagrams (figure 105). Work to an approximate girdle and profile the shape of crown and pavilion, allowing for a completed proportion of one third to two-thirds above and below the girdle but this need not be a standard measurement. Deviations will occur during cutting and working out the depths of parallel facets. Much will also depend on the size of the pre-form and to avoid wastage and a great deal of grinding it may be desirable to introduce extra rows of facets. The essential factor is the retention of the main facet angles in their respective positions.

It is essential to orientate the pre-form correctly on the dop for insertion into the chuck, particularly where there is an alignment groove or other securing device. The long central axis of the stone must correspond with index positions 64 and 32 in order to make use of the related index numbers shown in the diagrams.

Cutting Sequences

Directions for the remaining two styles will be brief since much of the required information can be obtained from the diagrams at this stage, since technical expertise will have been acquired through the challenge of cutting parallel facets in the Emerald Cut. Once the girdle outlines have been formed and carefully trued on the lap the crown and pavilion facets will be a repetition of the shape in a series of step cuts.

THE KITE SHAPE

This is the cut corner style which is a variation of the Kite Cut with the upper point on the long axis replaced by a flat girdle edge at right-angles to the centre line, requiring an extra index position (figure 110). Use two cutting stages.

The Girdle

Check the dopped stone for correct orientation with required index positions and cut the five-sided girdle at 90 degrees. In order to obtain perfect symmetry at both sides of the long central axis, cut each side alternatively a little at a time and carry out repeated checks. The girdle outline will establish its own proportions as cutting proceeds at the stated index position.

Crown Facets

Cut and polish the table, using the adaptor at 45 degrees. Cut five girdle facets, at 55 degrees, of equal widths and accurately aligned at each index position. Remember to finish on the finer cutting lap.

Reset the angle to 42 degrees and cut the five main facets to border the table. With larger stones the table area may still be greater than desired and in such cases an extra row of narrow table facets can be cut at approximately 27 degrees.

Retain the last angle and start to polish the series of crown facets in reverse order on the appropriate lap. The girdle edge can be polished when the pavilion facets have been cut and the girdle width has been reduced.

Carry out transfer dopping sequences to cut reverse facets and set the dop to align the stone at the correct index positions in the chuck of the facet arm.

Pavilion Facets

Index the same positions as used for the crown and cut five girdle facets at 63 degrees. As the facets spread towards the girdle check that the girdle thickness is

KITE CUT

Fig 110

Cutting order 1. Cut 5 girdle sides at 90°
              2. Cut and polish table. Follow with crown and pavilion sequences

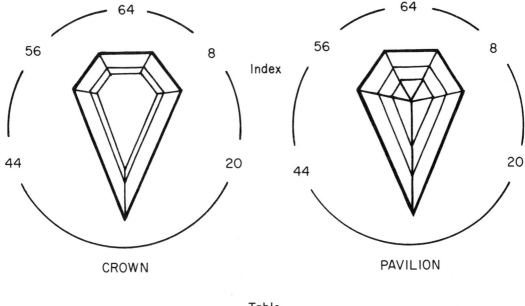

CROWN   PAVILION

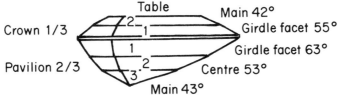

Additional crown table facet
can be added at 27°

running parallel at each face and take care not to over-cut. Find the correct positions on the lap to make any adjustment in alignment.

Cut the middle row of facets at 53 degrees, parallel to the first set and meeting exactly at each junction round the stone.

The last of the pavilion facets are cut at the main angle of 43 degrees and form the off-set culet point at the five facet junctions and the elongated tapering ridge along the central axis.

Polish the pavilion facets in reverse order and finally complete the stone by polishing the narrow girdle edge at 90 degrees.

THE KEYSTONE SHAPE

Dop the pre-form on either the crown or pavilion end, whichever portion is to be cut first. It is essential that the head of the dop and wax does not impede shaping of the girdle so a good clearance must be allowed when dopping on the table because the outline shape of the stone tapers.

Use two cutting stages throughout and refer to the cutting diagrams for correct index positions and orientation.

The Girdle

Cut the girdle shape at 90 degrees and square up the four sides. Do not make the stone too long and narrow in proportion to the width or the second row of crown facets will meet in a point at the table. A similar position will arise on the pavilion. Adjustment to the proportions must be made at the initial shaping of the girdle, cutting at index positions 64 and 32, to reduce the length.

Crown Facets

Cut and polish the table in the usual way, then cut four girdle facets at 55 degrees. The heights will need adjusting each time a change is made from the long sides to the ends.

Cut the four main facets at 42 degrees and check parallel alignment. With all step cut stones if the girdle is out of square the position on the lap will determine parallel facet rows. This will be located by a little trial and error period and repeated checks. As with the Kite Cut, an extra row of narrow facets can be added at the table if the stone is too large.

Polish the crown facets in reverse order to retain the previous setting for the first row.

Transfer to a new dop and orientate the stone in correct index positions.

Carry out a check by lowering the stone onto the lap surface and aligning the girdle at 90 degrees.

Pavilion Facets

It should be noted that the two end facets cut quickly in comparison to the two long facets and care must be taken not to overcut, particularly on the last two.

Cut the broad girdle facets at 63 degrees until a suitable girdle thickness is reached. Cut a second row of facets at 53 degrees. The main pavilion facets are cut at 43 degrees to form the culet point.

Polish all the pavilion facets, followed by the girdle edges.

THE KEYSTONE CUT   *Fig III*

Cutting order 1. Cut 4 girdle sides at 90°
               2. Cut and polish table. Follow with crown and pavilion sequences

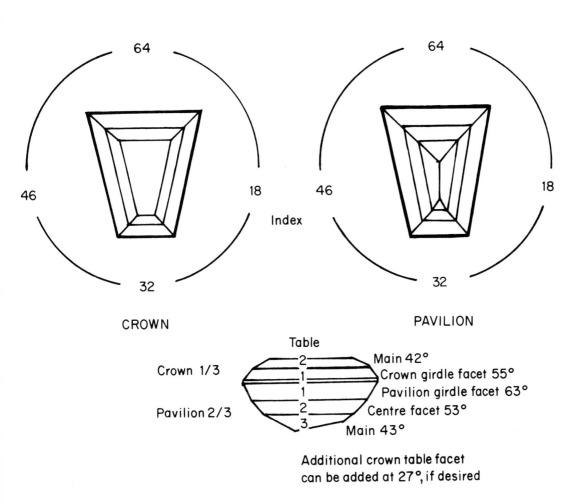

CROWN   PAVILION

Table
Crown 1/3   2——— Main 42°
                 1 ——— Crown girdle facet 55°
                 1 ——— Pavilion girdle facet 63°
Pavilion 2/3   2——— Centre facet 53°
                 3——— Main 43°

Additional crown table facet
can be added at 27°, if desired

Appendices

TABLE 1

Comparative Scales of Hardness

	Mohs' Scale	Approximate Knoop values
Talc	1	Not given
Gypsum	2	61
Calcite	3	141
Fluorite	4	181
Apatite	5	483
Orthoclase	6	621
Quartz	7	788
Topaz	8	1190
Corundum	9	2200
Diamond	10	8000

Relative Hardness of Abrasives

	Based on Mohs' scale	Approximate Knoop rating
Aluminium oxide	8–9	2000
Silicon carbide	9–10	2480
Boron carbide	9–10	2760
Diamond	10	8000

TABLE 2

Immersion Fluids

Many of the immersion fluids which can be used in testing crystals for possible flaws are poisonous and are best avoided by those not familiar with the use of chemicals of this nature. Among the simpler fluids with less risk are:

Fluids	Refractive Index
Water	1.33
Paraffin (kerosene)	1.45
Olive oil	1.47
Turpentine	1.47
Glycerine	1.47
Mineral oil	1.48
Oil of cedarwood	1.51
Oil of cloves	1.54
Oil of anise	1.55
Refractol	1.56
Oil of cinnamon	1.59

Most of the dangerous immersion fluids occur in a higher R.I. range but many of the fluids mentioned above will reveal the presence of pronounced flaws even in crystals of high R.I. when examined in a beam of light.

TABLE 3

Solutions of Convenient Densities for Testing Specific Gravities of Gem Minerals

Solution	Specific Gravity
Bromoform, diluted with toluene to density of quartz gems	2.65
Bromoform, undiluted	2.90
Methylene Iodide, diluted with toluene or bromoform to density of pink tourmaline	3.06
Methylene Iodide, undiluted at room temperature	3.32—3.33
Clerici Solution, diluted with distilled water to density of sapphire	3.99

Clerici Solution is a concentrate of soluable salts having a varying density depending on saturation and temperatures. It should be diluted only with distilled water. Capable of testing gems of high specific gravity such as corundum.

Most density testing solutions are poisonous, and Clerici Solution has an unpleasant reaction on the skin. Such solutions should be handled with extreme caution and used under suitable conditions. The solutions are also susceptible to colour changes and often lose their efficiency when stored for long periods or exposed to light.

TABLE 4

List of Specific Gravities for Some Gem Minerals

Alexandrite	3.71–3.72
Almandine garnet	3.95–4.40
Andalusite	3.15–3.17
Apatite	3.17–3.23
Aquamarine	2.68–2.73
Corundum	3.90–4.00
Synthetic corundum	3.98
Demantoid garnet	3.82–3.85
Diamond	3.52
Dioptase	3.28–3.35
Epidote	3.25–3.50
Emerald	2.69–2.75
Fluorite	3.18
Hessonite garnet	3.65
Kyanite	3.65–3.68
Morganite	2.80–2.90
Peridot	3.34
Pyrope garnet	3.65–3.70
Quartz	2.65
Synthetic rutile	4.25
Spessartite garnet	4.12–4.20
Spinel	3.58–3.90
Synthetic spinel	3.61–3.65
Spodumene	3.17–3.19
Topaz	3.53
Tourmaline	3.00–3.12
Yttrium aluminium garnet	4.60
Zircon high type	4.67–4.70
Zircon low type	3.90–4.10

TABLE 5

Main Angles Considered to be Suitable Guides for Planning a Series of Facet Cuts

Gem Mineral	Crown main	Pavilion main	Hardness (Mohs')	Refractive Index	Critical angle
Andalusite	43	39	$7\frac{1}{2}$	1.62–1.64	38
Apatite	43	39	5	1.64	38
Beryl	42	43	$7\frac{1}{2}$–8	1.56–1.60	39
Chrysoberyl	37	42	$8\frac{1}{2}$	1.75–1.76	35
Corundum	37	42	9	1.76–1.77	35
Dioptase	40	40	5	1.64–1.71	37
Epidote	36	42	$6\frac{1}{2}$	1.73–1.77	35
Fluorite	41	45	4	1.43	44
Garnet	37	42	$6\frac{1}{2}$–$7\frac{1}{2}$	1.73–1.88	34–35
Kyanite	40	40	5–7	1.71–1.73	36
Peridot	43	39	$6\frac{1}{2}$–7	1.65–1.68	37
Quartz	45/42	43	7	1.54–1.55	40
Spinel	37	42	8	1.71–1.73	36
Spodumene	43	39	7	1.66–1.67	37
Topaz	43	39	8	1.63–1.64	38
Tourmaline	43	39	7–$7\frac{1}{2}$	1.62–1.64	38
Zircon high	35	41	7–$7\frac{1}{2}$	1.92–1.98	31
Zircon low	37	42	$6\frac{1}{2}$	1.78	34

Note : Rigid adherence to main angles is not absolutely vital and a few degrees variation is permissible in some stones to meet particular requirements providing pavilion angles do not fall below critical angles. The critical angles shown in the table, based on the refractive indices of the listed minerals, denote the limits for total internal reflection of the incident light rays. As the refractive index increases the critical angle is reduced. Pavilion angles cut lower than the critical angle will cause the light rays to pass out of the stone and a lifeless gem or one of considerably reduced brilliance will result.

TABLE 6

Suitable Polishing Agents

Gem Mineral	Polishing Laps	Polishing Compounds
Andalusite	Tin	Tin oxide, Linde A
Apatite	Tin, tin-type metal, vinyl	Linde A
		Tin oxide
Beryl	Tin	Linde A
	Vinyl	Cerium oxide, tin oxide
Chrysoberyl	Tin	Linde A
	Copper	Diamond micron size 1
Corundum	Tin, vinyl	Diamond micron size 3
	Copper, lead	Diamond micron size 1
Epidote	Tin	Tin oxide
	Vinyl	Linde A
Garnet	Tin	Linde A
Peridot	Vinyl, tin	Linde A
Quartz	Tin, lead, vinyl	Linde A
	Acrylic (Perspex, Lucite)	Cerium oxide, tin oxide
Spinel	Tin	Linde A
	Lead	Chrome oxide, tin oxide
Spodumene	Tin	Tin oxide, Linde A
	Vinyl, lead	Linde A
Topaz	Tin	Linde A
	Vinyl	Linde A, cerium oxide
Tourmaline	Tin, lead	Linde A, tin oxide
	Vinyl	Cerium oxide, Linde A
Zircon	Tin, vinyl	Linde A

The polishing laps and compounds given above are recommended by many cutters and have been proven in practice, but where problems arise other combinations can be tried and may well be successful.

Suppliers of Lapidary Equipment and Materials

UNITED KINGDOM

M.L. Beach (Products) Ltd, 41 Church Street, Twickenham, Middlesex.

Caverswall Minerals, The Dams, Caverswall, Stoke-on-Trent, Staffs.

Craftorama, 3 Church Cowley Road, Oxford.

Derwent Crafts, 50 Stonegate, York.

H.C. Evans & Son, (Eltham) Ltd, 171 Main Road, Sidcup, Kent.

Gemrocks of Holborn Ltd, 7 Brunswick Shopping Centre, London WC1.

Gemset of Broadstairs, 31 Albion Street, Broadstairs, Kent.

Gemstones Limited, Hull, North Humberside.

Glenjoy Lapidary Supplies, 19/21 Sun Lane, Wakefield, West Yorkshire.

Hirsh Jacobson, 91 Marylebone High Street, London W1.

Kernowcraft Rocks & Gems Ltd, 21 Pydar Street, Truro, Cornwall.

Lynhill Lapidary Ltd, Huddersfield Street, Galashiels, Scotland.

Manchester Minerals, 420 Manchester Road, Heaton Chapel, Stockport, Cheshire.

Massie Lapidary, 108–110 Holme Lane, Sheffield.

Mineralcraft, 1 The Knoll, Crown Hill, Rayleigh, Essex.

Norgems, 38 High Street, Sandbach, Cheshire.

Scotrocks Partners, 9 Park Road, Glasgow.

Tideswell Dale Rock Shop, Tideswell, Derbyshire.

Trilobite, 37 Carlisle Close, Church Meadows, Winsford, Cheshire.

Wessex Gems & Crafts, Longacre, 121 Downs Road, South Wonston, Winchester.

USA

Allcraft, 22 West 48th Street, New York, N.Y.10036.

American Handicraft Co., Inc., 20 West 14th Street, New York, N.Y.10011.

Anchor Tool & Supply Co., Inc., 12 John Street, New York, N.Y.10038.

Anoziro Jewelers, 4002 North Stone Avenue, P.O. Box 3988, Tucson, Arizona.

Baldwin-Taylor Hardware & Rock Shop, 4301 Jefferson Highway, New Orleans, Louisiana 70121.

Diamond Pacific Tool Corporation, 24063 W. Main Street, Barstow, CA92311.

Geode Industries Inc., 106–108 W. Main, New London, Iowa 52645.

Gilman's, Hellertown, PA 18055.

International Gem, 15 Maiden Lane, New York, N.Y.10038.

Lapribrade Inc., 8 East Eagle Road, Havertown, Pennsylvania 19083.

Lapidary Center, 4114 Judah Street, San Francisco, California 94122.

Highland Park Manufacturing (Division of Musto Industries Inc.), 12600 Chadron Avenue, Hawthorne, California 90250.

Lortone Division of the Carborundum Company, Seattle, Washington 98107.

MDR Manufacturing Co., Inc., 4853 Jefferson Blvd., Los Angeles, CA 90016.

Ran-co Products, Granada Hills, California.

Ultra-Tec. Stanley Lapidary Products, Santa Ana, California.

CANADA

D. Sustrik Enterprises Ltd, Edmonton, Alberta.

Bibliography

Collecting and *Polishing Stones*, Herbert Scarfe, B.T. Batsford, London, 1970.

Comprehensive Faceting Instructions, D.L. Hoffman, Aurora Lapidary Books, USA, 1968.

Cutting and Setting Stones, Herbert Scarfe, B.T. Batsford, London, 1972.

Discovering Lapidary Work, J. Wainwright, Mills & Boon, London, 1971.

Facet Cutters Handbook, E.J. Soukup, Gembooks, California, USA, 1962.

Faceting for Amateurs, G. & M. Vargas, Desert Printers, California, USA, 1969.

Gemcraft, Lelande Quick and Hugh Leiper, Pitman and Chilton, London and Philadelphia, USA, 1960.

Gem Cutting, J. Sinkankas, Van Nostrand Co., USA, 1962.

Gemmologists' Compendium, R. Webster, N.A.G. Press, London, 1964.

Gems and Gemmology, C.J. Parsons and E.J. Soukup, Gembooks, California, USA, 1961.

Gems, their sources, descriptions and identification, R. Webster, Butterworths, London, and Shoe String, Hamden, Connecticut, USA, 1962.

Gemstones, H.G.F. Smith, 1952. Revised edition, Chapman & Hall, London, 1973.

Gemstones of North America, J. Sinkankas, Van Nostrand Co., USA, 1972.

Gem Testing, B.W. Anderson, Heywood & Co. Ltd, London, 1958.

Minerals and Man, Cornelius S. Hurlbut Jnr, Thames & Hudson, London, and Random House, New York, 1969.

Minerals and Rocks in Colour, J.F. Kirkaldy, Blandford Press, London, 1963.

Minerals, Rocks and Gemstones, Rudolf Borner, Oliver & Boyd, Edinburgh, and Dufour, Chester Springs, Pennsylvania, USA, 1962.

Pebbles as a Hobby, Janet Barber, Pelham Books, London, 1972.

Practical Gemmology, R. Webster, N.A.G. Press, London, 1966.

Practical Gemstone Craft, Helen Hutton, Studio Vista, London, 1972.

Rock and Gem Polishing, E. Fletcher, Blandford Press, Press, London, 1973.

Rock Collecting and Making Semi-precious Jewellery, Ron Warring, Stanley Paul, 1972.

Standard Catalogue of Gems, J. Sinkankas, Van Nostrand Co., USA, 1968.

The Art of the Lapidary, F.J. Sperison, Bruce Publishing Co., Milwaukee, USA, 1950.

The Gem Kingdom, Paul E. Desautels, Macdonald & Co. (Publishers) Ltd, London, 1971.

The Lapidary Manual, Herbert Scarfe, B.T. Batsford, London, 1975.

The Mineral Kingdom, Paul Desautels, Hamlyn Publishing Group, London, 1969.

Working with Gemstones, V.A. Firsoff, David & Charles, Newton Abbot, Devon, 1974.

Index